To
dr. Krzysztof Jasiewicz

Flenderski
September 5, 1997
Gdansk

MONITORING ECONOMIC TRANSITION

Monitoring Economic Transition

The Polish Case

GEORGE BLAZYCA
Department of Economics and Management
University of Paisley

JANUSZ M. DĄBROWSKI
Gdańsk Institute for Market Economics

Avebury

Aldershot • Brookfield USA • Hong Kong • Singapore • Sydney

Published by
Avebury
Ashgate Publishing Limited
Gower House
Croft Road
Aldershot
Hants GU11 3HR
England

Ashgate Publishing Company
Old Post Road
Brookfield
Vermont 05036
USA

British Library Cataloguing in Publication Data

Blazyca, George
   Monitoring Economic Transition
   I. Title II. Dąbrowski, Janusz M.
   338.9438

   ISBN 1 85972 068 4

Library of Congress Catalog Card Number: 95-60402

   Typeset by
   Alison Forsyth
   Department of Economics and Management
   University of Paisley

Printed and bound by Athenæum Press Ltd.,
Gateshead, Tyne & Wear.

Contents

Figures and tables

Acknowledgements

Presenting the results of what is essentially a Polish research programme to an English speaking audience is not without problems and we owe our greatest thanks to those who have helped us to overcome those difficulties. Throughout the course of this project we have relied heavily on the support of the secretarial staff of the Department of Economics and Management at the University of Paisley. This is an opportunity to thank all those who helped but we certainly owe a special "thank you" to Alison Forsyth who patiently and with unswerving good humour tackled successive revisions of heavily edited text, gradually shaping it into the final product. We are also indebted to those others around us, especially our families - the Dąbrowski's of Warsaw and the Blazyca's of Glasgow - who have tolerated our absences as we struggled to assemble this book. We must thank our contributors for their patience in responding to editors' whims in revising earlier chapters and for their hard work in carrying out the basic research upon which the book is based. Finally, a special thanks is also owed to our translators.

Contributors

Professor George Blazyca

Associate Head of the Department of Economics and Management at the University of Paisley, Scotland, and author of many reports and papers on Polish economic and business developments, including, *Poland's Next Five Year: The Dash for Capitalism*, (Economist Intelligence Unit Ltd, Special Report No. 2110, London, 1991).

Dr Janusz Dąbrowski

Vice-president of the Gdańsk Institute and Director of its Warsaw branch, associate professor of economics at the Warsaw School of Economics. Dr Dąbrowski is an active researcher with many papers on enterprise behaviour. He has been a consultant to the OECD, World Bank and Polish Privatization Ministry, and on the board of the Warsaw based *Powszechny Bank Kredytowy*.

Dr Krystyna Gawlikowska-Hueckel

Senior researcher at the Gdańsk Institute and associate professor in European Integration at Gdańsk University. Dr Gawlikowska-Hueckel has researched at the European University Institute in Florence and is the author of many books and papers on the process of European integration and regional investment risk. She runs a Gdańsk Institute research project on regional investment risk in Poland.

Mr Maciej Grabowski

Vice-president of the Gdańsk Institute and lecturer at the University of Gdańsk. Dr Grabowski has been a consultant to the OECD, IFC and World Bank. His major interests include private sector development, tax policy and the informal sector. He manages a Gdańsk Institute project on small business development and tax policy in the transformation process.

Dr Mirosław Gronicki

Senior research fellow at the Gdańsk Institute and a former Fulbright scholar at the University of Pennsylvania. Dr Gronicki specialises in macroeconomic forecasting and is heavily involved in producing the quarterly Gdańsk Institute growth forecasts.

Dr Janusz Lewandowski

Co-founder of the Gdańsk Institute and of the liberal-conservative part the, Congress of Liberal Democrats (now merged with the Democratic Union to form the Freedom Union party). Dr Lewandowski served as minister of privatization in the government led by fellow "Gdańsk liberal", Krzysztof Bielecki in 1991, and again in 1992-93 in the government headed by Mrs Hanna Suchocka.

Professor Leszek Pawłowicz

Professor of economics at the University of Gdańsk, vice-president of the Gdańsk Institute, Director of the Gdańsk Banking Academy and member of the board of *Bank Gdański*. Professor Pawlowicz is an expert on banking and finance and runs the Gdańsk Institute's research on Bank - corporate debt restructuring.

Dr Zbigniew Polański

Assistant professor in banking at the Warsaw School of Economics, senior research fellow at the Gdańsk Institute and consultant to the National Bank of Poland.

Dr Jan Szomburg

Co-founder and president of the Gdańsk Institute, member of the prime minister's advisory council on privatization and on the steering committee of the mass privatization programme. Dr Szomburg chairs the boards of *Bank Gdański* and the Polish Development Bank. He has written widely on privatization and was the author in 1988 (with Dr Janusz Lewandowski) of the first mass privatization scheme in Eastern Europe.

Dr Bohdan Wyżnikiewicz

Senior researcher at the Gdańsk Institute and manages the Institute's work on short-term forecasting. Dr Wyżnikiewicz was formerly president of the Central Statistical Office (GUS) and has served with the United Nations Economic Commission for Europe (UNECE). He has been a consultant to the IFC and World Bank.

Introduction

Almost as soon as "shock therapy" was applied in Poland in 1990 a newly established independent research organisation, the Gdańsk Institute for Market Economics (GIME), began painstakingly to monitor its economic impact. The Institute made it its business to get to the heart of the transformation process through a unique series of investigations observing at first hand change and development. This volume, the first collection of "Gdańsk Papers", brings to a wider audience the real impact of the transformation taking place in Poland in the 1990s.

Researchers, students, journalists and business people will find in this book a unique account of four years of momentous change, material tracing the big issues - state firms' and how they adapted to new conditions, privatization, the development of the small business sector, banking reform and the problem of how to deal with balance sheets filled with "bad debts", Poland and the obstacles standing before its ambition of being a full member of the European Union by the year 2000. The material presented in this book, for the first time published in English, will, we hope, lead to a better understanding of the transformation process not only in Poland but, given the commonality of problems, across the region.

1 The Gdańsk Institute for Market Economics: An insider's account

Janusz M. Dąbrowski

The Gdańsk Institute for Market Economics (GIME) was established in 1989 on the initiative of a group of Gdańsk liberals who had been political opposition activists in the 1980s. The institute was the first independent, non-governmental, and entirely private scientific research institution in Poland and probably in the whole of East-Central Europe. It emerged on the basis of a desire for independence, political freedom and the freedom to create a new economic reality. Such thinking had united young Polish academics working at universities, scientific institutions or conducting business activities, who came together and embarked on building, in the old political system, the framework of a free economy.

Towards the end of the 1980s, following the demise of communism and the removal of legal and political barriers to independent institutions in Poland, the institute was formally established. Its main founders included Janusz Lewandowski, its first president before being appointed minister for privatization in 1991 and then again in 1992-93, and Jan Szomburg, a Solidarity expert in the 1980s who became the GIME president in 1991. The institute began work with a team of a few researchers in a small office in the centre of Gdańsk. Within five years it had become an establishment providing jobs for more than thirty full-time and almost twenty part-time employees. It also developed co-operation links with a network of a dozen or so locally based contributors. In 1990 a Warsaw branch of the institute was set up. Two years later the institute's Lublin branch was established. The next major development came in 1993 with the setting up, within the institute structure, of the Gdańsk Banking Academy, educating staff for the financial sector in Poland.

Since its inception, the GIME has fostered the restoration of a market economy in Poland. Its activities concentrated on preparing the legal and economic infrastructure, analyzing the process of systemic change, providing an education in market economics for academics, businessmen and journalists, publishing the results of studies and research projects in the form of booklets and press articles, staging seminars and conferences. As a non-profit organization, the institute received funds for carrying out these projects in the form of grants, donations and support for commissioned research. The institute's major sponsors and benefactors includes the Konrad Adenauer Stiftung, the Ford Foundation, the Centre for International Private Enterprise, the UK government Know-How Fund, the German Marshall Fund, the World Bank, the Foundation of Polish German Collaboration, the Polish Development Bank and the Polish privatization ministry.

The GIME has specialized since its inception in a comprehensive, in-depth monitoring of the transformation process. It was the first scientific and research institution to monitor the process of state-enterprise adjustment to new conditions, to examine privatization, small business and capital market developments. This pioneering research, widely disseminated to many Polish and foreign agencies, later became a model for other research institutions which built on the GIME experience. To date, the results of the institute's analyses have been used by such institutions as the World Bank, the International Finance Corporation, the OECD, and as regard Polish agencies, the industry ministry, the central planning office and the Polish chamber of commerce. Moreover, the institute's publications are distributed to a large number of other centres, universities and economic organizations both in Poland and abroad. An increasing community of academics and journalists reporting on transformation processes in Central Europe quote the findings of the GIME.

The institute's research projects largely concentrate on monitoring the most crucial aspects of systematic transformation and economic development. Their continuity (most projects are long-term) together with their blend of quantitative and qualitative techniques give them a unique character. Special attention is given to the qualitative aspect of transformation. This is because of the variety of social and economic phenomena at stake and the diverse behaviour of various actors involved in the stormy process of transition to the market economy. These are simply impossible to grasp by means solely of traditional statistical research methods.

Because of the nature of its research and its high quality the GIME has become recognized both in the country and abroad as providing first-hand knowledge on systemic transformation in Poland, offering its own independent assessments on economic development and making recommendations to help solve the most acute problems posed in the transition period. Over the 1990-94 period some of the institute's researchers were recruited by government agencies, while many others became consultants to domestic and foreign institutions. The institute's influence may also be measured by the number of invitations to conferences and seminars, as well as a constant flow of proposals from abroad to engage in joint research projects.

The papers prepared for this book, following a general introduction and overview by Blazyca, bring together some of the key findings and results of studies carried out during the first five years of the "systemic revolution" in Poland. They summarize projects spanning six broad areas of research. Their selection is not accidental. It is our intention to present an overview of the systemic changes taking place in Poland between 1989 and 1994 as illustrated by the findings of our regular studies over this period.

Blazyca sets the scene with his account of the major issues in a paper specially prepared as an introduction for the Western reader. We then move to a consideration of the macroeconomy and draw attention to the forecasting work of the Gdańsk Institute. From then our interest shifts to the micro level. We report on enterprise adjustment in the state sector before examining privatization and private business development. The inadequacies of the financial sector have often been pointed to as a major impediment to economic development in Eastern and Central Europe and this becomes the next focus of attention. Lastly, broadening the issues once again, we consider some of the very contentious issues relating to Poland's place in Europe as we approach the new millennium.

Each of the contributions from Poland is based on original GIME research. The paper on "Forecasting the Polish Economy", stems from the first research project to yield a regular quarterly evaluation of economic developments, an estimation of major economic variables and the projection of business trends for the six months ahead. These analyses are published well ahead of official data released by government agencies, the central statistical office (GUS) and the central planning office (CUP). This Gdańsk research is, at least up to the end of 1994, the only source of regular up-to-date Polish GDP estimates and projections. This project is based on co-operation with Deutsches Institut für Wirtschaftsforschung (DIW) a Berlin-based research institute with more than sixty years of experience in this area. With DIW know-how, advice and support the quality of the Gdańsk institute's work could attain a high quality level in a very short time.

Another paper, that by Szomburg raises fundamental questions concerning political and social barriers to systemic transformation. It focuses on the relationships between the efficiency of reforms and the political foundation which may guarantee support for the changes being implemented. The Polish situation reflects here the adverse consequences of an unstable political arena. As a result of having neither a strong nor consolidated political base supporting the transformation of the economy social opinion can become dominated by anti-reform movements trading on a popularity stemming from uncertainty, fears and frustrations. The fact that the political parties which advocate the process of systemic transformation have a very limited impact on social attitudes poses a real threat of slow-down or even of discontinuity. The Szomburg paper is part of a broader project dealing with the identification of barriers to transformation.

Other chapters tackle public sector issues and privatization. Dąbrowski summarizes almost four years of research into the responses and adjustment of state-owned enterprises to new operating conditions. The author discusses the pace and intensity of adjustment and the influence of factors like company size, industry sector and market position. Here the Gdańsk studies are unique. They are the only systematic record based on a steady sample of enterprises, a regular monitoring of adjustment processes from the start of transformation.

The paper on privatization of state-owned enterprises by Lewandowski, a former privatization minister, outlines the philosophy of privatization in Poland, together with an account of the basic approaches utilised. The development of the privatization process is also discussed.

Research on small business development began in 1990 and was then repeated regularly, providing a basis for more informed views on the sector's internal growth rate as well as barriers to its development. The special feature of this research, by Grabowski, lies in the analyses of private entrepreneurs' own responses prepared on the basis of direct interviews.

Another research project, that concerning monetary policy in the transformation period, is based on National Bank of Poland (NBP) and central statistical office data supplemented with the GIME's own analyses of processes and developments. Monetary policy has a significant role in the process of stabilizing the economy and checking inflation as well as being a factor fostering economic growth. The paper by Polański explaining these issues reviews both the effectiveness of monetary policy instruments over 1990-94 together with an evaluation of the performance of the entire financial sector.

A similar range of problems is reviewed in the paper on the banking sector by Pawlowicz. It provides a comprehensive account of banking development during the period 1990-94. It also discusses the major barriers to further development of the banking sector at the same time assessing developments in upgrading state-owned banks, their privatization, as well as the development of private banks and the opening up of Polish markets to foreign banks. Pawlowicz also looks closely at the implementation of the debt restructuring law dealing with the problem of bad debts. This unique research permitted an immediate insight into the effects of debt restructuring in reducing state-owned enterprises' liabilities vis-a-vis banks where non-performing assets held by state-owned banks were re-capitalized by the state treasury. Non-performing loans pose one of the most serious problems in transition economies. The impact of the Polish debt restructuring exercise is therefore intriguing both from the point of view of continuing systemic reforms and with pure research in mind.

We conclude the volume with a paper by Krystyna Gawlikowska-Hueckel who places Poland in a wider European context and examines some of the problems that will need to be overcome if Poland is to become a full member of the European Union in a reasonable time span. Fostering and sustaining economic growth in countries like Poland aspiring to join is the key issue: lack of growth threatens to release some destructive forces which could also be immensely damaging to Western Europe. Poland and its place in Europe is likely to be a major concern for all Europeans as the decade draws to a close.

Because of the concise scope of this book we have left to one side many other issues, such as privatization of municipal enterprises, local government, capital market development, investment risk evaluation, issues that have been investigated by the institute for several years. We hope that another opportunity will arise at a later date to present some of this research to the wider public.

2 Monitoring economic transformation

George Blazyca

Economic policy and performance since 1989

In August 1989, as the first Solidarity government, led by Tadeusz Mazowiecki, came to power, some 40 years of Communist rule and Soviet style economic management ended in Poland. Central economic planning, which had in any case by that time more or less seized up, was abandoned and the move to the market started. This transformation was planned by the newly appointed finance minister, Leszek Balcerowicz, whose famous "Balcerowicz plan", a shock therapy to extinguish Poland's hyperinflation, came into effect on 1 January 1990.

The new government's policy intentions were both clear and ambitious. The aim was to create as speedily as possible a Western style market economy. Following what later became standard IMF advice on the economics of transformation the Polish programme had three strands: stabilization, restructuring and privatization. But in late 1989 when the monthly inflation rate was running at over 30 per cent it was clear that stabilization was the priority task. Thus, though Mazowiecki and Balcerowicz were both committed to privatization, the new government's economic policy became best known because of its firm deflationary stance. Some have argued that it was too firm for too long (Rosati, 1991a, 1991b, Poznański, 1993).

The Balcerowicz plan rested on several pillars: a highly disciplined approach to public spending and tight control over the state budget; a sharp devaluation of the złoty to a new fixed rate against the $US to create sustainable "internal convertibility", to instil confidence in the domestic currency and encourage a shift of resources into exports; and a tough tax based incomes policy, which became known as the *popiwek* tax (*podatek ponad-normatywowych wynagrodzen - ppw*), to break price-wage inflationary push, a pressure very much a feature of Polish economic life and one that threatened to explode as subsidies were reduced and prices liberalized.

Another crucial aspect of "Balcerowicz" was its insistence on opening Poland to the world economy. As trade barriers were dismantled Poland was for a time (1990 and into 1991) perhaps one of the world's most open economies. Strong domestic producer pressures for protection were resisted more successfully than is commonly the case in the West. Later, when Poland together with Hungary and the then Czechoslovakia, struck an association agreement with the EC, "the Visegrad three" won the argument that there should be asymmetry in the rate of tariff barriers reduction, the EC acknowledging the Polish and East European need for a longer breathing space for adjustment.

Prices, wages and taxes

Liberalization was a major plank of the Balcerowicz plan and almost all prices in Poland are determined by the market. Of course, many monopolistic producers exercised muscle especially during the early part of 1990 in marking up prices. But strong import competition and the recession also had an impact on price formation. Moreover, in at least one or two cases the anti-monopoly commission intervened in the price setting process. By 1995 the category of "official prices" set by the state (*ceny urzedowe*) remained in force for few items, typically the prices charged for services provided by the major public utilities such as energy and transport.

As the last vestiges of central planning disappeared so state firms came to enjoy complete wage setting freedom. But this was a freedom disciplined by the *popiwek*. If state enterprises increased their wages bill by more than an allowable proportion of monthly price inflation they were liable to a steep wages tax. The coefficient determining the allowable increase was initially set (in January 1990) at a highly restrictive 0.2 but was later raised to 0.6 and on occasion, usually following sharp bouts of industrial unrest, was made equal to unity. By 1992 the *popiwek* was under great pressure from trades unions and it became plain that it might not for much longer serve as an effective first defence against an inflationary wages surge. The search for an alternative anti-inflationary defence centred on the development, with trades unions, of the so-called "enterprise pact", essentially a wide ranging social contract through which the authorities hoped to speed up privatization. Private firms were exempt from the *popiwek* on the grounds that "real owners" could be relied on to exercise self-discipline over excessive wages growth. Thus privatization was viewed, by Solidarity governments, as the best long run substitute for the *popiwek* and the best anti-inflation policy.

Real earnings fell significantly over the period of the Balcerowicz plan though the raw statistics overstate the actual decline: in the earlier period, say the 1980s, real earnings growth was no guarantee of greater purchasing power.

Table 2.1
Earnings and cost of living growth 1989-93
(% growth on previous year)

	1989	1990	1991	1992	1993
Nominal earnings*	292	398	71	39	34
Cost of living	260	558	71	43	35
Real earnings	9	-24	0.0	-3.6	-1.0

*   Average monthly net nominal earnings
Sources: Mały Rocznik Statystyczny 1994, (GUS, Warsaw), p.95.

The "budget sector", where incomes are provided directly by the state for public services, also lost out, after 1990, against the business or "enterprise sector".[2] In 1991 and in 1992 the typical net monthly wage in the public sector was 92 per cent of that in the enterprise sector, declining in 1993 to 88 per cent. Public sector earnings pose a major political challenge to the Polish authorities who have been required by law to ensure their indexation against average earnings. In 1992 the authorities failed to maintain the appropriate parity: to have raised wages any further would have resulted in budgetary complications at a time when delicate discussions were under way with the IMF. The failure to index fully was ruled illegal by the constitutional tribunal but the government "excused" itself by promising to make good the shortfall at a later date with privatization bonds.

As part of its transformation to Western style economy Poland has created a Western style system of direct and indirect taxation.

Progressive personal income taxes at three rates (20 per cent, 30 per cent and 40 per cent increased to 21, 33 and 45 per cent from 1995, after a political battle between government and president) were introduced at the start of 1992 - virtually no income tax was paid before - although enterprises did pay taxes on their wages fund.[3] The antiquated and often byzantine system of "turnover taxes", taxes which the authorities levied at a multitude of rates on factory and wholesale prices, was replaced in July 1993 by a system of VAT. Enterprises pay a uniform profits tax (40 per cent in most recent years) and state firms also paid (or were supposed to, enterprise tax arrears contributed to a piling up of firms' indebtedness) a tax on assets known as *dywidenda*. This however was due to be phased out in 1995 alongside the *popiwek* tax on wages and earnings growth.

It is worth noting that there is little evidence that the rapidly expanding private sector has paid much in the way of taxes over recent years (see Grabowski, chapter 7, p.114 in this volume). Its impressive development was therefore supported by the heavily taxed state sector.

Following prices and exchange rate liberalization the currency black, for so long a poisonous feature of day to day life in Poland, vanished. Of course there is undoubtedly a large "grey economy" of unrecorded economic transactions. It is difficult to know the precise scale of informal economic activity but the Polish statistical office research centre has estimated that in 1993 it accounted for złoty 340,000 bn, a sum equivalent to just over 21 per cent of GDP.[4] One of the major problems in moving to a comprehensive new model of taxation is that the scope for tax evasion is considerable while the ability of the authorities to ensure compliance is limited.

Output and inflation

During 1990, 1991 and well into 1992 the output side of the economy took the brunt of the deflationary force of the Balcerowicz plan. Between 1989 and 1992 GDP fell by around 17 per cent and industrial production by 33 per cent. Inflation however was reduced to manageable proportions, from 251 per cent on average in 1989 and 586 per cent in 1990, to 70.3 per cent in 1991, and 43 per cent in 1992. The success of the anti-inflationary thrust of Balcerowicz is better seen through the monthly growth in prices: the rate fell from 11 per cent in 1990 to only 3.1 per cent during 1992.

Table 2.2

GDP, industrial production and inflation 1989-92

(% change on previous year)

	1989	1990	1991	1992
Real GDP	0.2	-11.6	-7.6	2.6
Industrial Production	-0.5	-24.1	-11.9	0.0
Consumer prices	251	586	70.3	43.0

Sources: Mały Rocznik Statystyczny 1992; Rzeczpospolita, 6 February 1993, *IMF*, (press release, 5 August 1994).

In the very early 1990s, in a period when the macroeconomic shock was immense, Polish economic statisticians began a fundamental reconstruction of measurable economic categories, shifting from the Material Product System (MPS) to the UN System of National Accounts (SNA). It was not long before Gdańsk Institute researchers began also to re-examine macro developments through more conventional GDP type variables abandoning the old central planning Net Material Product (NMP) view of the economy. Gronicki and Wyżnikiewicz explain in chapter 3 of this volume the background to the Gdańsk approach. Through the optic of their reconstruction of economic data they also tell the story of Polish macroeconomic developments in the early 1990s. They track a 1992 economic recovery which rested on consumption and exports but which was in danger, in their view, of running out of steam before the general recovery of the world economy came to the rescue in 1993. We return to more recent developments later.

Social responses

Of course, as might be expected, economic policy as forcefully implemented as the Balcerowicz plan creates political strains and social tensions. Moreover, against the backdrop of experiments with a newly discovered democracy internal difficulties soon surfaced (farmers' protests in 1990, a bitter motor industry strike in August 1992 and a month long miners' strike in December 1992) which also contributed to an unfortunate though essentially misplaced external image of Poland as politically unstable. It is remarkable however that the Solidarity "parasol" held for as long as it did given the speed and the depth of the recession that the country fell into in early 1990. The Mazowiecki government, and Balcerowicz in particular, were well aware that a situation where the leading trade union did not move to defend the immediate interests of its members could hardly endure for long. The number of strikes officially recorded in 1990 amounted to just 250 involving 115,687 workers. By 1991 those figures had increased to 305 and 221,547 respectively and in 1992, a politically much more explosive year some 6,362 strikes were recorded involving 730,000 workers.[5] Unemployment meanwhile began to grow at a fast pace, from an officially recorded zero rate in 1989 to 6.3 per cent of the economically active labour force by end 1990, 11.8 per cent by end 1991 and 13.6 per cent by end 1992.[6] Full employment in the old system meant, in reality, considerable under-employment and it is frequently argued that in the new system the unemployment total exaggerates by a wide margin the true state of joblessness. But all countries suffering from high unemployment have some which is more apparent than real, perhaps amounting to 10 or 20 per cent of the total according to economists from the Warsaw School of Economics (see *Transforming the Polish Economy*, 1994, p.92). There can be little doubt that unemployment in Poland was and remains a chronic social problem.

Gains and disappointments

Balcerowicz plan achievements

By mid 1990 the government of Tadeusz Mazowiecki responded with a mild easing of economic policy but there was to be no substantial policy adjustment until May 1991 when the złoty, which had appreciated considerably in real terms much to the detriment of exports, was devalued. All through this period a growing popular disenchantment with the economic situation of the country became evident. And even when the economy turned the corner with a resumption in growth in 1992 there was little evidence in Poland of any "feel-good" factor. More surprisingly perhaps, as that growth accelerated to 3.8 per cent in 1993 and perhaps 4.5 per cent in 1994, the degree of social malaise remained high.

Nevertheless, if mistakes were made in applying for too long a deeply restrictive macroeconomic policy (something that might not be accepted by most of the contributors to this volume), the Balcerowicz period produced real gains for the cause of creating in Poland an effective economic mechanism. One of its central achievements was the elimination of shortage. More or less chronic shortage, queuing, informal and grey market activity were continual features of central planning wherever it existed. The liberalization of prices in Poland immediately ended shortage. If this simply displaced one rationing device by another there would perhaps be little to trumpet. However price liberalization in Poland was accompanied by a flurry of mainly private sector activity which aimed to meet, albeit depressed, market demands. Even if privatization was slower than hoped the private sector, as we report in more detail below, was on the move. There can be little doubt too that the elimination of the $/złoty black market and the US dollar as Poland's parallel currency was a major achievement, as was the elimination of the multitude of exchange rates for various transactions that had previously existed. All of these measures helped pave the way to currency reform in January 1995 when the authorities could feel confident enough over inflation to introduce a new złoty which removed four zeros from existing banknotes.

A disappointing enterprise adjustment?

Alongside the gains there were of course some disappointments. One was the tardy response of many state firms to new economic conditions. This is an area where the researchers of the Gdańsk Institute have performed a sterling service by getting inside the state enterprise and tracking, almost from day one, its responses to new economic conditions. The first reaction of largely monopolistic producers facing declining demand was to raise prices and restrict output. And though state producers must have contributed to the export success story in 1990 (see again below) this was nevertheless in the context of a steep fall in overall production. It was not until early 1992 that clearer signals appeared suggesting that state enterprises were at last achieving increases in sales. This was the overall picture but the Gdańsk research reported in this volume by Dąbrowski in chapter 4 highlights the complexity of the situation across state firms. The author usefully reminds us that the successful adjustment of public enterprise remains crucial to the success of the reform process in Poland. Just how well then, the author asks, have state firms adjusted?

Certainly, and as might be expected, private firms responded more quickly to the new environment. Again, as one would expect, large state monopolists, especially those in heavy industry, had the biggest problems. The immediacy with which firms faced competition also affected responses. State sector enterprise in consumer goods sectors were the first to meet competition head on and many showed that they could rise to the immediate challenge. Often, in 1990, workers, unions and management came together within the firm to devise adjustment strategies and the "Bermuda triangle" (an unhappy and debilitating cocktail of the short-term interests of unions, workers' councils and managers) was not at that time the general characteristic of state firms that some would have us believe. Later, however, an "insider" problem did emerge and became clearest perhaps with respect to privatization, an issue explored in detail by Szomburg in chapter 5. Thus, the research described in detail by Dąbrowski points to a frequently healthy initial adjustment of state firms to new conditions where those firms were in consumer goods sectors and faced competition. Their reaction however was based essentially on new marketing efforts - few had the resources to enable them to invest in longer term adjustment strategies. No one will need to be persuaded that large state monoliths were and remain in trouble: here the only realistic course appears to be to court a combination of new private sector investment alongside public sector (EU and governmental) support for adjustment strategies with reasonable time horizons.

A poor pace of privatization?

The Gdańsk Institute is unequivocal in its support of privatization and two of its founder members, both writing in this volume , Jan Szomburg and Janusz Lewandowski, played a major role in shaping privatization policy. Lewandowski with Szomburg were leading figures behind Poland's unusual mass privatization scheme and Lewandowski himself served two stints as minister responsible for privatization. Both write with an insider's insight to the range of problems that exist. Szomburg elegantly draws out the wider contours of the factors shaping privatization focusing in particular on the role of firm insiders and how they have influenced the real pattern of privatization. Lewandowski too is in no doubt that in Poland privatization has remained very much in the hands of the enterprise. In Poland actual privatization was very much shaped by the strong tradition of worker-management and the enterprise was a much more important arena than parliament in moulding policy. This clearly caused the authorities some consternation at various points in time from 1989. Many readers will be interested to discover, from Szomburg, that even during the almost religiously "hands-off", market-oriented Balcerowicz period, the authorities considered "re-nationalization" as a device to assert control over state assets prior to their speedy disposal. The point however was not pressed because, as Szomburg tells us, the government felt it had its hands full in ensuring that its restrictive macro-economic policy did not spill over into the streets. The moment was lost and Polish privatization developed with its decidedly "autonomous" character: the enterprise insiders calling the shots. Thus, although the major privatization route in Poland was through the "liquidation" then disposal (usually to insiders) of the firm, and this was successful as far as it went, most of the leading actors and commentators view privatization results as unexpectedly disappointing. They are, on the other hand, cheered by the equally unexpected rapid growth in the small private business sector.

The "nomenklatura" privatization that occurred spontaneously from 1989 and favoured enterprise managers was, on the whole, argues Szomburg, a positive phenomenon: for all its moral deficiency it did result in a sharp boost to private business activity. With the passage of a short interval in time it also, he believes, "sparked the ownership instincts of workers" helping to shape the boom in management-employee buy-outs that characterised the major part of privatization in Poland from 1990 to 1994. Thus, no matter the legal situation, the fact of the state's weak ownership rights gave room to manoeuvre to those with privatizing energy and ambitions. In 1995, when it looked as if a post communist government was about to engage in the "re-nationalization" of its assets, Szomburg's concern was that this would become an end in itself, and, a privatization substitute. This may be too pessimistic. If the state can avoid being captured by new lobbies then a period of consolidation of ownership rights and the emergence of well defined industry policy (anathema, it must be said, to most Gdańsk Institute authors) aiming for the restructuring of major sectors may be no bad thing.

It is worth recounting the major developments in Polish privatization. After many revisions and considerable parliamentary acrimony a privatization bill was passed on 13 July 1990. This opened the way for a variety of privatization devices including so-called "capital privatization", whereby successful larger state enterprises, after detailed valuation studies (usually conducted at that time by Western consultants and accountants), might be publicly floated. This conventionally individual approach, tried and tested in the UK, proved to be both expensive and time consuming. As 1990 drew to a close only five firms were on the brink of flotation on the Warsaw stock exchange. Jeffrey Sachs (1993), the leading Western adviser to Leszek Balcerowicz, made much of the fact that, at this rate, privatization of the Polish stock of some 6,779 state enterprises would take, to put it mildly, a considerable time. Even with acceleration in the pace of "capital privatizations" the period from 1990 to September 1994 saw only 124 firms transformed in this manner.[7]

Alongside "capital privatization" a process of privatization through liquidation also operated which produced much more significant ownership changes in the fast growing small business sector of the economy. But it soon became clear that these two routes alone would imply privatization dragging on for many decades and leave Poland, once the pioneer in reform, lagging behind its neighbours in East and Central Europe. With the passage of time a number of other privatization styles were adopted including sectoral and mass privatization. Lewandowski describes them in chapter 6.

Sectoral privatization was conceived of as a device for action on an industry-wide basis. It was reasonably effective in drawing some Western investors into Poland. But it also doubled as a substitute for industrial policy with occasional conflicts between the competing visions for sectoral development of various parties especially the industry and privatization ministries. Some of the most notable cases of Western inward investment included General Motors (with Warsaw's FSO cars), International Paper (with the giant Kwidzyn cellulose-paper plant), Fiat (involved with FSM cars) and Lever (the Pollena soap powders enterprise).

It was during the presidential election campaign of summer-autumn 1990 that Lech Wałęsa raised the political stakes over privatization, pointing to the need for its "acceleration" but at the same time giving another twist to its politicization. A discussion on speedy mass privatization soon followed. Initial plans for mass privatization (*Program Powszechnej Prywatyzacji - PPP*) were developed by Janusz Lewandowski in his first stint as privatization minister during the period of the Bielecki government in 1991. But the inconclusive general election of that October and the paralysis of government that followed under the premiership of Jan Olszewski (December 1991 to June 1992) froze further developments. It was only when the government led by Hanna Suchocka was formed in mid 1992, with Lewandowski back at privatization, that a renewed mass privatization momentum was generated.

In early August 1992 the government published the draft proposals for mass privatization which were to take almost two and a half years to reach the statute books. These centred on the creation of a layer of around 15 investment funds (*Narodowy Fundusze Inwestycyjny - NFI*) to hold shares in, and manage the affairs of, 400 to 600 leading state firms.[8] The number of firms involved proved to be one of several contentious issues and the final package arrived at towards the end of 1994 brought the number of participating companies down to the lower end of the original band (444). The *NFI* are to be jointly run by a consortium of Western and Polish managers under a majority Polish board with Polish chairmen (all, as it turns out are male, a gender bias that will surprise few and which is evident also among new private entrepreneurs as Grabowski, in this volume, demonstrates).[9]

In summary, the pace of privatization over 1990-94 was never as fast as had been hoped. Mistakes were acknowledged in trying to model Polish privatization on a UK type case-by-case approach. The most successful privatization style turned out to be insider based "nomenklatura" privatizations followed by management-worker buy-outs of liquidated companies. Privatization meanwhile became highly politicized, a football in the political game. In society at large privatization enthusiasms began to flag. In this situation it was a Solidarity government headed by Mrs Hanna Suchocka that, in 1993, proposed an "enterprise pact" as a device to win greater workplace support for privatization.

This pact is viewed by Szomburg as a discredited "social corporatism" but once again that judgement may prove unduly pessimistic. The pact's emergence was undeniably evidence of the need felt by the state to give privatization a firmer central steer. From 1993 post-communism promised to take up where Solidarity left off with plans for mass commercialization of state enterprises to reassert the state's ownership rights in a prelude to sectoral restructuring and privatization. Only time will tell whether the pessimists are right to believe that post-communism is intent on de-railing privatization.

The private business boom

One of the undoubtedly impressive achievements of the transformation under way in Poland since 1990 was the tremendous expansion of the "home-grown" private sector - the small business sector described and discussed in another piece of exemplary Gdańsk Institute research by Maciej Grabowski in his aptly titled chapter, "Learning by doing". The dynamic pace of this dimension of transformation is perhaps most readily gauged by the share of GDP attributable to the private sector. In the late 1940s, before the economy was extensively nationalized, the private sector accounted, reports Grabowski, for 70 per cent of GDP. Midway through the Polish experience of central planning, by 1968, that share had fallen to 20 per cent. For 1989 Dąbrowski, in chapter 4, puts the figure at 18 per cent accelerating by 1993 to 60 per cent, not too distant from the 1948 share.[10]

Poland perhaps enjoyed what appeared to be a start over other transforming economies in that it had a private sector poised to expand beyond the limits artificially imposed by central planning. Its private sector on the threshold of change in 1990 accounted for 33 per cent of employment as compared to Hungary's 25.3 per cent and Czechoslovakia's tiny 6.3 per cent share. Nevertheless in all three countries the private sector expanded vigorously in the years that followed. Grabowski however draws attention to critical structural weaknesses of the Polish private sector which may have a bearing on its ability to develop further. It is an exceptionally small scale and poorly capitalized business sector: the average employment per "enterprise" in the "unincorporated sector" is only 1.8. On the other hand the "incorporated" private business sector represents larger and more dynamic enterprise but here Poland supports fewer businesses per capita than does either Hungary or Czechoslovakia, presumably an indication of untapped potential combined with a hint, perhaps, of the existence of barriers to development. Another particular feature of the Polish small business scene is its "autarchy": it trades, it seems, much more intensively with itself than is the case for either of the other countries surveyed where private-state interactions are more common. Other observers of the economic scene in Poland note illegality as a characteristic features of Polish small business. Not only is there much tax evasion, but other legal provisions such as the labour code, health and safety legislation and trade union provisions are regularly flouted.

Once again Gdańsk research projects have gone into the sector and it is through these that we can describe some of its main features. It appears that the typical Polish entrepreneur is male, middle-aged, well-educated, with previous managerial experience (and contacts). It also transpires that firms are, not surprisingly, locally based, serving local customers with very few involved in exports (this suggests that the 1990 exports boom was largely the result of adjustments in a much maligned state sector). It is interesting too to note that Polish private business is as self-oriented as any elsewhere believing that privatization is good medicine for its suppliers but less convinced that privatization which leads to increased competition in its own product markets is a good thing.

Grabowski discovers that Polish entrepreneurs succeeded in a process of "learning by doing" at a time when energetic business people could fairly easily find a place on the market. But now, he suggests, skills are becoming more important, including marketing and finance skills. Here however the budding entrepreneur meets the Polish banking system and what may also be a major barrier to business development. Grabowski notes that most entrepreneurs surveyed do not use banks for credit purposes - 70 per cent of small businesses surveyed in 1990-91 had made no attempt to raise bank loans. At this point it is worth referring to Polański's critical review (chapter 8) of the banking system. The story for Polański is relatively disappointing: the banking system is not performing the functions it should be if it were properly to support economic development. The deficiency lies largely with an institutional inability, he argues, to assess risk and allocate capital. Like most other Gdańsk Institute authors, Polański, is afraid that post-communism may slow financial sector reform with a deleterious impact on future economic development. But this may again be over pessimistic. Pawlowicz, in his account of bank reform in chapter 9 shares some of these concerns but points to a considerable Polish success story with respect to a major banking problem common to all formerly planned economies - the restructuring of bad debts accumulated especially sharply by larger state firms as their markets shrank or disappeared.

The Polish enterprise-bank debt restructuring scheme represents an innovative and unique approach to dealing with a particularly tricky problem and we describe its main features below after outlining the major elements of banking reform in the period since 1989.

Banking reform

Polish banking reform began in 1989 with the restructuring of the "monobank", the National Bank of Poland (NBP). Nine independent but state owned banks were carved from the NBP.[11] They were "commercialized", that is, transformed into state owned joint stock companies, with privatization in mind. The National Bank of Poland was then charged with traditional central banking functions and has achieved an impressive independence in discharging its duties.[12] Thus banking reform appeared to move quite well, the first privatization of a commercialized bank, that of the Poznan based *Wielkopolski Bank Kredytowy SA*, took place in 1993. The second attempt at privatization was not so successful, at least in political terms. When the Katowice based *Bank Śląski* was privatized in January 1994 the 13 fold increase in share prices on first trading, alongside conspicuous insider-dealing, resulted in a political furore and a bitter struggle between coalition members, which brought down one finance minister and one deputy finance minister.

If mainstream bank privatization proceeded rather slowly there seems to have been more success in dealing with the thorny problem of how to purge bad debts from bank balance sheets. The Polish authorities implemented a debt clean up operation which Pawlowicz believes was highly effective. Some other informed observers are, it should be noted, more cautious and believe that while banks' balance sheets may be cleansed the problems which caused enterprise indebtedness in the first place will not disappear (see *Transforming the Polish Economy*, 1994, pp. 324-6).

Essentially the scheme (made law in the Financial Restructuring Act of 19 March 1993) operated by demanding that state banks should find ways to clean up their balance sheets *themselves* with once for all support provided by the state. The alternative, to create as in the Czech Republic, a new institution to hold all bad debts, a "bank for bad debts" was rejected as too costly, too time-consuming and lacking the desirable changes in future lending behaviour without which any bank reform would be, at best, half baked. In Poland the banks had first to identify their bad debts. They then had to decide how to deal with them, choosing between restructuring, debt-equity swaps or selling on the debt. At same time, with EC (PHARE) support, an intensive and badly needed programme of top quality and practical debt assessment training was initiated. As one organiser of the programme related "a young bank employee from Szczecin might be sat down for a number of weeks with someone from a Western bank/accountancy concern next to him".[13] Banks also reorganized themselves developing new structures and departments to avoid the renewal of bad debt. Lastly, all this had to be achieved to strict deadlines with banks told that they had to meet new capital adequacy guidelines by the end of March 1994.

The programme seems to have generated a greater sense of commercial responsibility. Banks reduced lending and became considerably more cautious - perhaps helping to explain some of the difficulties in securing loans frequently complained of by Polish business. The end result was however that state banks involved in the programme became fully covered for bad loans and they understood that this governmental bale-out was a once only event: prudent lending would have to be the rule for the future.[14] Thanks to the implementation of a decentralized solution, leaving banks to sort out debts themselves, backed by once-off government financial support and EC funded retraining it may be that many of the major state banks are in a much healthier position from which to conduct business in the late 1990s.

Pawlowicz points to some remarkable achievements in the banking sector which are largely the result of the debt restructuring programme. First, it successfully introduced the idea of investment banking based on a responsible assessment of risk. Second, enterprises got into the habit of looking outside for professional restructuring help. Third, and perhaps most important of all, there appears to have been little political lobbying for soft loans and where it occurred the "pressure exerted was rarely successful" (see p.152). When one recalls that the programme was implemented during the first period of post-communist government this is surely some evidence to counter the notion that post-communism must always fall prey to one or other of the lobbies which political opponents argue post-communism will always cultivate. For Pawlowicz however the most important outcome was that lenders holding 50 per cent of debt were granted the right to enforce restructuring while simultaneously administrative coercion on lenders - a long-standing feature of central planning - disappeared.

Yet despite these gains both Pawlowicz and Polański are concerned that the banking system may yet fail to support enterprise development in the future. Polański takes the view that if the factors that have supported economic growth thus far dry up the financial sector will still be too poorly developed to contribute to economic recovery. Pawlowicz believes that "the Polish banking system is in crisis" (p.159) despite recent achievements. Even if their fears of post-communism are exaggerated it is worth bearing in mind that the benefits of the debt restructuring programme were felt only by state banks. Elsewhere banks may be in trouble. "Lifeboat" schemes to insure the financial system from collapse may increase credit costs and further discourage borrowers. But the crux of the matter is what happens in enterprises and in the quality of the bank-enterprise nexus and here the jury is still out.

Foreign trade adjustments and relations with the EU

Exports and imports

No assessment of the Polish economy since 1989 would be complete without a comment on international relationships and the trading scene. One of the most striking features of the Balcerowicz period was the 1990 exports boom. Another was the growth of private sector trade - at least as far as imports were concerned - while yet another was the extremely rapid switch in trade away from the former Comecon region towards the West and in particular towards the EC, Comecon ceased to function in 1991 when trade at world prices and in hard currency became the norm.

Taking into consideration the uncompetitive structure of the economy Polish exports' performance has been generally surprisingly good in the period of economic transition since 1989. The year 1990 saw exports growth (in dollar value terms using National Bank data) of 43.4 per cent taking the export total to $10,863 million and generating a trade surplus of $2,214 million. A further 17.5 per cent growth in 1991 pushed exports to $12,760 million. In 1992 exports increased by 9.7 per cent to $13,997 million. In 1993 however exports were extremely poor, falling in dollar value by 3 per cent and prompting a further devaluation of the złoty. But by 1994 European recovery came to Poland's aid and exports performance was, once more, surprisingly strong.

As for imports, recession and devaluation in 1990 ensured their growth would at first, compared to exports, be limited: they increased by 17.9 per cent to $8,646 million. But by late 1990 and into the first half of 1991 real złoty appreciation (nominally fixed at the then "anchor" exchange rate of złoty 9,500 per $) generated a substantial increase (47 per cent) in imports taking the total import bill to $12,709 million. In the first major amendment to economic policy since January 1990 the authorities yielded a złoty devaluation in May 1991. A further devaluation occurred in February 1992 giving exports another boost. Imports, as expected, slowed in early 1992 but by the second half of the year once again increased strongly. With 1992 export earnings of $13,997 million and imports up by just over 6 per cent to $13,485 million the country had a trade surplus of $512 million ($51 million in 1991). But as economic growth picked up in 1993 imports began to be sucked in at a fast rate and export weaknesses became more apparent. According to NBP data Polish trade fell into a substantial deficit of $2.3 billion in 1993, the first deficit recorded by the bank since before 1989. In 1994, thanks mainly to recovery in the German economy, the exports resurgence was, as noted earlier, extraordinarily strong.

Table 2.3
Trends in foreign trade[a]
(convertible currency trade, $ mn)

	1989	1990	1991	1992	1993	1994[b]
Exports	7,575	10,863	12,760	13,997	13,585	16,532
Imports	7,335	8,649	12,709	13,485	15,878	17,278
Balance	240	2,214	51	512	-2,293	-746

[a] Note that trade flows are also estimated by the Central Statistical Office, GUS, through customs declarations and those estimates differ, sometimes markedly, from the payments data reported here by the National Bank.
[b] Own estimate for year based on NPB data for first nine months recording exports of $12,182 million and imports of $12,628 million.

Source: Balance of payments data from the National Bank of Poland reported in Statistical Yearbooks and in *Rzeczpospolita*, 12 December 1994.

Poland and the European Union

Over the short period, 1989-92, Polish trade structure underwent a remarkable shift: as Comecon collapsed the EC became Poland's major trading partner. The EC share in Polish exports increased from 32.1 per cent in 1989 to 57.9 per cent in 1992 while the EC share in Polish imports rose from 33.8 per cent to 53.2 per cent. Germany replaced the former Soviet union as Poland's number one trading partner in a trade reorientation that took Poland in the early 1990s back to a trade pattern more characteristic of 1929.[15] The bulk of this adjustment took place before Poland's association agreement with the EC (signed in March 1992) had any time to take effect. That agreement was intended to improve Polish access to EC markets and while no doubt it has had some impact frictions between Warsaw and Brussels are disturbingly frequent. Some examples of the difficulties that arise are recounted below.

Table 2.4
EC share in Polish trade 1989-92
(% shares)

	1989	1990	1991	1992
Exports	32.1	46.8	55.6	57.9
Imports	33.8	42.5	49.9	53.2

Source: GUS data reported in *Rynki Zagraniczne*, 12 July 1993.

In November 1992 the Commission imposed temporary anti-dumping duties on imports of East European steel tubes. Poland was faced with an extra duty of 10.8 per cent, Hungary with 21.7 per cent and the then Czechoslovakia with 30.3 per cent. In March, EC countries decided to retain duties on some steel tube imports for a further two months. April 1993 saw the sudden imposition of restrictions on East European livestock exports to the Community on the grounds (spurious as far as the East Europeans were concerned) of evidence of foot and mouth disease in some livestock arriving in Italy from Croatia. Though these restrictions were largely lifted by July the Poles complained of lost export sales worth $30 million and pointed to the higher future cost of meeting (in their view discriminatory) new veterinary regulations despite the fact that Poland's last reported case of foot and mouth was as long ago as 21 years. Then, in a further turn of the restriction screw, the EC announced in mid July that minimum prices would be applied to Polish exports of sour cherries. This prompted an outraged Polish trade minister, Andrzej Arendarski, to complain that he awaited the next restriction to follow whatever EC fruit crop enjoyed a bumper harvest.

The commodity structure of exports is changing considerably. In 1980 the dominant export sector was the large electrical and mechanical engineering industry with 43.3 per cent of *all* export sales. This fell to 29.3 per cent in 1990 and was 27 per cent in 1993. Such a decline was inevitable following the collapse of Poland's captive, thirsty, uncompetitive and undiscriminating Comecon market. For the bulk of the post-war period to 1990 Poland's reputation as a modern industrial state rested on machinery and equipment exports to the former Soviet Union and Eastern Europe. But that sector's exports to the West were always marginal. Eurostat reports that machinery, equipment and transport equipment accounted for 11.2 per cent of EU imports from Poland in 1990, a share that changed little to 1992 when it was 12.6 per cent. EU data reveal that the bulk of Poland's exports to the region in 1990 were food and agricultural produce (21.4 per cent) followed by metals and metal goods (16.6 per cent), light industry products (13.1 per cent), fuel and minerals (12.1 per cent). By 1992 metals, light industry, food and fuel still accounted for 59.8 per cent of all EU imports from Poland. Hence the importance to Poland of access to markets in Western Europe which are politically sensitive. The slight that Poland feels when the European Commission seems too readily supportive of anti-dumping actions brought by EU producers also becomes readily understandable.

Table 2.5
Poland's trade balance with the EU by
major commodity group

	(ECU mn)	
	1990	1993
Metals	595.1	474.5
Food and agricultural produce	491.3	57.0
Fuel and minerals	483.9	270.5
Wood products	229.6	393.1
"Other" manufactures	125.1	352.8
Machinery and electronic equipment	-956.0	-1,803.3
Chemical products	-83.7	-762.2
Total (including others)	812.8	-2,145.5

Source: Eurostat data reported in Rynki Zagraniczne, 28 July 1994.

Krystyna Gawlikowska-Hueckel, in her contribution to this volume (chapter 10), "Poland and Europe", gives a broader context which helps locate, from a Polish perspective, some of these issues. She emphasises the importance to Poland of a real European commitment to wider membership of the Union and one that comes sooner rather than later but with a schedule that is *announced* immediately. Of course Polish economists are well aware of the major obstacles to membership, especially the structural ones like the CAP and the sheer underdevelopment of Eastern Europe. But there is a concern that the costs of adjustment are too heavily biased towards aspiring members and these, it should be remembered, are poor countries. Poland, to take the subject of this book, had a GDP per capita in 1993 equal to 10 per cent of the Union average. But great importance, for political reasons, is attached to a schedule for membership. This may help deflect the dangers of growing nationalism and other destructive "social pathologies".

Social and regional differentiation

A clear pattern of regional differentiation overlies existing and emerging social stratification. The unemployment map of Poland is the best guide to the new pattern of regional development. At mid 1994 the unemployment count reached 2,933,000, or some 16.6 per cent of the economically active labour force. Kraków (8.3 per cent unemployment) and Warsaw (7.7 per cent unemployment) are least affected. Poland's unemployment black-spots are found in the peripheral economies clustered around each other in the North East: Suwalki with an unemployment rate of 29.5 per cent, neighbouring Olsztyn with 30.7 per cent, Elbląg with 27.5 per cent and Ciechanów with 23.9 per cent. The Koszalin and Slupsk provinces just to the West of Gdańsk are other problem areas with 28.7 per cent and 30.7 per cent unemployed respectively as is the Pilski region immediately to the south with unemployment of 25.5 per cent. Wałbrzych, in the lower Silesian region, is another problem area with 27.3 per cent of the labour force unemployed.

Regions of high unemployment are characterized by one or more of the following: concentration of heavy industry, poor infrastructure and relative remoteness, towns and cities dependent on few, usually very large, employers. They are not the most attractive areas for inward investment and they are the regions where social unrest is likely to be most readily manipulated especially if it becomes apparent that the benefits of faster GDP growth are not fairly shared. It seems likely that the government will need to develop a firmer and clearer regional policy for the medium term and this is a policy area likely to win increased international support. Long term unemployment (over one year) is a serious problem, accounting for a large proportion (over 40 per cent) of the total. Over one half of those unemployed (54.6 per cent) are not entitled to benefits. Clearly, as economic growth and restructuring proceeds some of these problems will be eased but unemployment is bound to continue to be regionally concentrated in slower growing parts of the country. Nor is any immediate unemployment reduction in prospect: it is more likely to level off and stick at around 16.0 per cent through the mid 1990s.

The political scene since the September 1993 election

The party political scene in Poland is lively, complex and still considerably fragmented although likely to be less so in the period that lies ahead. Prior to, and during the great upheaval of 1989 Polish political life was fairly easy to follow and interpret: Solidarity made an initially smooth transition from opposition to government while the Communist Party and communist authorities simply faded away. But it was not long before the inherent tensions within the unstable Solidarity mix exploded into a myriad of mainly right of centre political parties and "grouplets". This, and the economic austerity of 1990-92, fostered a widespread social unease which aided the recovery of "post-communism" in 1993. Constant feuding in the Solidarity camp(s) also played its part in the emergence of the post-communist SLD-PSL government after the September 1993 general election.[16]

Table 2.6
Polish prime ministers and governments 1989-94

Tadeusz Mazowiecki	Solidarity	September 1989	First Solidarity government
Jan Krzysztof Bielecki	Congress of Liberal Democrats (KLD)	December 1990	Sejm still dominated by communist party
General election		September 1991	
Jan Olszewski		December 1991	Brought down in May 1992 by President Wałęsa after a bitter fued on "de-communization"
Waldemar Pawlak	Polish Peasants' Party (PSL)	June 1992	Unable to form a workable coalition
Hanna Suchocka	Democratic Union (UD)	June 1992	Brought down by a Solidarity trade union MPs' no confidence vote in June 1993
General election		September 1993	
Walemar Pawlak	PSL/ Democratic Left Alliance (SLD) coalition	October 1993	

Notes:
KLD   Kongres Liberalno-Demokratyczny
SLD   Sojusz Lewicy Demokratycznej
PSL   Polskie Stronnictwo Ludowe
UD   Unia Demokratyczna

The election result was greeted with alarm and dismay by the post-Solidarity groups which were confounded by an electoral mechanics that worked against small parties. Many Polish observers predicted dramatic shifts in economic policy, not least a general caving in of the new coalition to popular pressures. Inflation, some warned (there are hints of this in contributions to this volume), would once again accelerate and the economic transition might even be de-railed. Domestic business looked on cautiously and slightly nervously. So too did Western investors, at that time still (judging from investment flows) relatively unimpressed by Polish economic possibilities. But the post election reality differed substantially from the mainstream expectations of the disappointed parties. If it became more complex, with new and unanticipated political fault lines, there was also much less to be alarmed about. Luckily for the new authorities the economic recovery that had glimmered in 1992 when GDP appeared at first to increase by 0.5 per cent continued to gather pace. Indeed, the early estimate of 1992 growth proved to be severely under-estimated: later assessments suggested growth of 2.6 per cent in that year.

What were the major tensions on the political scene in 1994-95? First, the two coalition partners cohabited in an uneasy compromise where differences were not slow to surface. Second, the government was given to bouts of intense conflict with the president, very often instigated or manipulated by Wałęsa himself. Third, the social-industrial scene remained volatile: strikes could suddenly erupt and when they did, could last for stubbornly long periods.

Yet, after surviving its first full year in power, the coalition showed that it possessed enough resilience to last a good deal longer. Indeed, were it not for the presidential election due to take place in late 1995 the government, helped by a growing economy, looked set to consolidate its position and see out a full term of office, taking it to the next general election in 1997.

The presidential campaign unavoidably muddied the waters. Leading personalities from the coalition looked certain to participate in that contest the outcome of which would undoubtedly tip the delicate balance of power between coalition and presidency. If Wałęsa were to be returned with a strong vote he might feel vindicated in pushing the coalition to breaking point, to a point perhaps where a new general election might be called. Indeed, by late 1994 some commentators wondered whether Wałęsa might not push the coalition to breaking point even sooner, perhaps using as a pretext a presidential veto over some issue such as the constitution or the state budget for 1995. If however none of this comes to pass and the post-communist SLD were to capture the presidency then the coalition (or at least one of its pillars) would of course be immeasurably strengthened and the PSL peasants' party would have little choice but to accept a more constrained role in government. Opinion polls are notoriously fickle and although Wałęsa trailed during most of 1994 it would be unwise to write off his chances of retaining his current post.

The short history of Poland's coalition government revealed two political parties engaged in an almost constant struggle for the upper hand. A job-sharing compromise reached just after the election concentrated economic decision-making power in the hands of the SLD, the party with its roots in urban Poland and with the closest connection to the old Communist Party. The PSL, firmly based in the countryside and stoutly defending peasant interests, provided the prime minister, Waldemar Pawlak, and reluctantly accepted exclusion from the two key economic posts - the ministries of finance and privatization. But since September 1993 the PSL, at times egged on by Wałęsa, lost no opportunity to challenge the post election settlement and to try to win greater influence over economic policy. With the appointment in May 1994 of Grzegorz Kołodko as deputy premier and minister of finance this became harder for the PSL. Kołodko, a determined and ambitious professional economist, was eager to make his mark on economic policy. Soon after taking office he proposed a medium term "Strategy for Poland", one of the features of which was the creation of a strong state treasury - managed by Kołodko. Nevertheless the PSL did not give up, continuing to behave opportunistically in trying to win greater economic policy influence.

The coalition also had constant problems with Wałęsa which seemed bound to intensify in the run up to the presidential election. Wałęsa's strategy was to divide the coalition partners. He aimed to create a public image of himself as a staunch anti-communist, not necessarily anti-government but certainly anti- its SLD wing. Although the PSL was for many years the sleeping partner of the Polish Communist Party the rural vote that it represents is one that Wałęsa clearly wanted to count on in the presidential election. Even if the PSL put up its own candidate for the presidency Wałęsa would hope to win PSL support in the second round, appealing to the basically Conservative and Catholic sentiments of Polish farmers. All of this suggested that government-president disputes would become increasingly focused on its SLD wing.

Outside parliament and presidency a different politics was also at work. Workplace protests remained very much a part of the Polish political scene. Major strikes could erupt unexpectedly as happened for example in the Belchatow power plant in April 1994, or in the Katowice steelworks in June and in the Warsaw steelworks in July of the same year: they could be lengthy and bitter - but rarely government threatening. The industrial scene, like party politics, is fragmented. The two leading trades unions, the OPZZ *(Ogólnopolskie Porozumienie Związkow Zawodowych* - literally, the All-Polish Congress of Trades Unions)[17] and Solidarity, the former with its MPs in the post-communist coalition, the latter with no formal political representation in the parliament elected in September 1993 but firmly anchored to "opposition", were at doctrinal loggerheads and found it impossible to co-operate at the national level. Despite coalition tensions the Pawlak government agreed that its line on industrial disputes should be one of non-intervention. Clearly, for major trouble spots in key state sectors this position was always going to be hard to defend but there was a serious intent to leave industrial disputes to owners-managers-workers to resolve. This, plus trade union fragmentation, in an economy that was in any case growing fast, made it unlikely that the coalition government would be brought down by a tidal wave of industrial unrest.

Post Solidarity parties had such a poor election in 1993 that parliamentary opposition was not something that worried the coalition greatly. But the fragmented Solidarity right was likely to re-construct itself in the run up first to the presidential, and then to the next general election. The Democratic Union party merged with the Congress of Liberal Democrats in early 1994 to form the centre-right Freedom Union *(UW - Unia Wolności)*, the leading post Solidarity party. Other mergers looked likely. The first major test of these new alliances was the presidential contest and their first hurdle to find suitable candidates. The political base that Wałęsa intended to fight from did not crystallize in 1994 although the Non Party Bloc for Reform *(BBWR - Bezpartyny Blok Wspierania Reform)*, the vehicle used by Wałęsa to try to win some parliamentary influence in 1993, still clung to life. The Freedom Union intended to field its own candidate with leading contenders Jacek Kuron (from the left) and Hanna Suchocka (from the right). The SLD looked likely to choose its leader Aleksander Kwasniewski whom opinion polls pointed to as the most dangerous threat to Wałęsa.

The worst fears regarding the impact that post-communism would have on the economy and business environment failed to be realized during 1994. Indeed the pace of recovery, if anything, accelerated while inflationary pressures remained under control - although it will be evident from some of the contributions to this volume that the Gdańsk Institute does not necessarily share this view. Looking further ahead, Kołodko's "Strategy for Poland" outlined a medium term framework which, judged from the perspective of a Western observer, appeared to be widely welcomed by domestic business. The IMF also gave its seal of approval. The strategy not only set out medium term economic targets but began to point more clearly to an underlying approach to economic problems which was more interventionist, less doctrinaire and surprisingly managerial. This was captured, for example, in proposals to "commercialize" from the start of 1995 very large numbers of state firms, bringing them under the responsibility of a strong state treasury, which *could* leave managers in firmer control over enterprise assets. This once again is a matter of some concern to the Gdańsk Institute as is evident from the comments of Szomburg and Lewandowski in their contributions to this book. But even Szomburg recognizes the problem caused for effective enterprise governance by the dispersion of responsibility for state firms among numerous central bodies, ministries and banks as well regional authorities. The Kołodko idea appeared to be to simplify and clarify ownership-control links in a prelude to privatization. Commercialization would spell the abolition of the workers' council, a body widely regarded as a serious impediment to restructuring. The Kołodko style of economic management appeared to lean more heavily towards tight control by firms' directors than to workers' participation. Szomburg however fears that commercialization will become a substitute for privatization and authors from the Gdańsk Institute would probably describe the Kołodko strategy rather differently as an attempt to return control to the "centre".

The "Strategy for Poland" had as its major medium term macroeconomic goals:

single figure inflation (8.7 per cent) by 1997;
fast GDP growth (5 per cent per annum) with even faster exports (8 per cent) and investment growth (8 per cent);
constrained growth in consumption (3.5 per cent per annum);
real interest rates to be kept positive to encourage savings;
rate of exchange rate depreciation to track inflation.

Meanwhile, the strategy also highlighted a number of more institutional features:

1   a powerful state treasury to be created as ultimate and clearly defined owner of state assets;
2   the "commercialization", originally scheduled to take place from January 1995 but likely to be delayed, of most state owned enterprises so as to clarify precisely ownership title (currently often dispersed among state organs), to strengthen management and

remove the blocking power of workers' councils;

3 reform of the state pensions system to remove existing "structural" defects which could have an explosive effect on state spending;

4 for public sector workers the substitution of existing wage indexation measures by a process of wage settlement by individual negotiation with trades unions, preferably for multi year periods.

The Kołodko strategy appeared internally consistent but the forecast hinged on the maintenance in 1995 through to 1997 of the high investment and exports of 1994. Perhaps its major weakness was an over optimistic inflation projection. The assumption that wage pressures can be satisfactorily resisted by more clearly defined managerial authority and by new bargaining mechanisms is untested and perhaps unjustified.

If the pessimists were confounded by the strength of recovery in 1994 and the vigour of the policy initiatives published since Mr Kołodko took over finance they were however correct in anticipating problems with privatization. The exceedingly slow implementation of the mass privatization programme disappointed many. While the SLD run ministry of privatization was keen to press on with the scheme the prime minister delayed approval of the final tranche of enterprises to join the programme. Here was another opportunity for the PSL to challenge the SLD sway over economic policy and to stall a programme that the more conservative Peasants' Party did not embrace wholeheartedly. But towards the end of 1994 the SLD demanded an end to PSL obstructionism over this matter and mass privatization came back on track for an early 1995 launch. The PSL unwillingness to go along with plans for the privatization of the tobacco and sugar sectors provided another opportunity for a bruising internal fight and the slowing down of a major restructuring programme.

Table 2.7
Strategy for Poland - major economic variables
(% growth)

	1994	1995	1996	1997	Performance 1994
GDP	4.5	5.0	5.2	5.5	4.7
Consumption	3.1	3.3	3.6	3.6	2.0
Investment	6.0	7.0	8.0	8.0	6.0
Exports	6.0	7.0	8.0	9.0	15.0
Imports	2.5	4.0	5.2	6.0	2.0
Real earnings	1.5	2.8	3.0	3.1	2.0
Prices	23.6	16.1	12.0	8.7	29.5
Unemployment % rate, end-year	17.2	16.7	15.6	14.0	16.0

Sources: Rzeczpospolita, 11-12 June 1994; Gronicki, M., and Wyżnikiewicz, B., *Estimation of main indications in 1994*, Gdańsk Institute for Market Economics, January 1995.

Prospects for the Polish economy

The regular flow of short term data published by the Polish authorities pointed in late 1994 to a recovery that was losing none of its momentum. Gdańsk Institute forecasters appeared broadly to agree (see Gronicki and Wyżnikiewicz, 1994). Growth was rooted in a dynamic private sector and fuelled on the demand side by a modest growth in consumption, more rapid investment growth and impressive exports growth. The "Strategy for Poland", the first governmental medium term policy statement to appear in recent years, may contribute to creating greater confidence in growth prospects. These are further reinforced by major developments on the international financial scene, especially Poland's stand by agreement with the IMF and the debt forgiveness package agreed with London Club banks in 1994 - the latter granted around the same 50 per cent debt relief on commercial debt that had been agreed with the Paris Club on official debt in March 1991. The major downside factor over the short to medium term future was the uncertainty unavoidably caused by the 1995 presidential election and the damage it might do to (especially foreign) investment intentions. There was thus the possibility that strong growth alongside the increased confidence that might flow from the adoption of a sound medium term programme, together with the much improved international financial scene might all combine to outweigh investor caution stemming from the inevitably noisy presidential election. That election need not de-rail Polish growth prospects. A plausible medium term scenario for Poland, in this author's view, might go as follows: GDP growth averaging 5 per cent per annum, fuelled by continuing strong investment and exports growth. Consumption will of course play a growth sustaining role but policy will successfully reinforce the trend to faster growth of savings and investment. The National Bank will continue to exert prudence over money supply growth and nominal interest rates will fall only in line with inflation.

Will robust medium term growth be seriously damaging to inflationary prospects? There are no grounds for alarm here although wage pressures, as several Gdańsk Institute authors note, need to be watched carefully. The following factors may help contain inflationary pressures: a strong finance minister committed to holding the line on pay and to staying out of workplace disputes; the intention too to strengthen managerial authority; and the fragmented trade union scene.

As inflationary expectations diminish there will be growing pressure to adjust downwards the crawling peg exchange rate arrangement which, in 1994, facilitated an automatic monthly złoty depreciation of 1.6 per cent, then 1.5 per cent and finally 1.4 per cent. But a certain amount of contest over this issue (and inflationary expectations) is evident between the finance ministry and National Bank. The latter tends towards a more guarded view on inflation. The Bank is also more single-mindedly engaged on an anti-inflationary crusade than is the finance ministry. Tensions between the two institutions help shape the exchange and interest rate regimes, or perhaps more accurately, help determine the timing of changes to these instruments. Over the medium term, złoty depreciation and interest rates will track falling inflation. With very strong exports growth during 1994 the trade balance case for any more dramatic exchange rate adjustment - a further devaluation - ebbed. In the longer term it is crucial that Poland remains on a high export growth track if new international payments obligations flowing from London and Paris club debt deals are to be met.

The research of the Gdańsk Institute helps to identify a number of other factors which are likely to have a critical bearing on Polish prospects and which any observer of the Polish scene would be well advised to keep in mind. The small private business sector, dynamic though it is, may soon reach credit and skill barriers that may be difficult to cross. The banking system may not develop fast enough a judicious credit allocating and monitoring facility. The reemergence of the "lobby" - whether agricultural or (less likely perhaps) heavy industrial - with its powers to capture government spending and patronage must also remain a danger. State owned enterprises need to generate or attract investment if they are to make any of the deeper adjustments essential to meet the new situation of intense competition they find themselves in. Poland must also find ways of attracting a much greater share of inward investment. A firm timetable for EU membership looks likely to be one of the single most important issues for the future and the failure to agree on one is likely to have immense consequences both economic and political. But most important, and perhaps potentially most dangerous, will be the damage that might be done to any successful transformation by social and regional disparities that grow in unrestrained manner.

Notes

1   My thanks to Professor Alistair Young and Dr Janusz Dąbrowski for comments on an earlier version of this paper. Any remaining errors of fact or judgement remain solely the responsibility of the author.
2   The "enterprise sector" covers units, regardless of ownership form, active in industry; construction; transport; communications; trade; forestry; electricity, gas, steam and hot water supply. The "budget sector" covers those units, mainly health and education, entirely dependent on the state budget.
3   A quasi-income tax, *podatek wyrównawczy*, (literally "equalising payment") did exist before 1992.
4   See, "Raport o szarej strefie: 340 bln złoty poza ewidencya", *Rzeczposolita*, 18 April 1994.
5   Annual statistical yearbooks.
6   *Biuletyn Statystyczny*, No., 9, (1994), (GUS, Warsaw), p.12.
7   "Sytuacja społeczno-gospodarcza kraju", *Rzeczpospolita*, 7 November 1994.
8   The *NFI* are typically formed from a partnership between Polish and Western banks, management consultants and Western fund managers. The 15 selected by late 1994, with some of their leading backers were:
     Polskie Towarzystwo Prywatyzacyjne (51 per cent Kleinwort Benson

Overseas, 49 per cent Polski Bank Rozwoju; *The Raiffeisen Atkins Consortium*; *Creditanstalt - SCG Investment Fund Management* (50 per cent Creditanstalt Investment Bank); *Yamaichi - Regent European Projects Poland*; *Girocredit-BRE*; *BPH-Invesco-Recovery Group*; *Westfund Consortium* (33 per cent Central Europe Trust, 22.22 per cent Charterhouse, 11.11 per cent Credit Commercial de France, 33.67 per cent Bank Zachodni); *KP Consortium* (24 per cent KPMG Peat Marwick, 20 per cent Bank Handlowy); *Hevelius*; *Hanseatic Investment Services* (ING Bank); *Eagle Management*; *The First Poland Corp/ONEX*; *Konsorcjum* (involving Barclays de Zoette Wedd, Company Assistance Ltd, Pekao SA); *Konsorcjum* (involving Lazard, Wielopolski Bank Kredytowy and others); *KNK/Reich & Tang*. Source: *Gazeta Wyborcza*, 19 December 1994.

9   The central idea underlying the *PPP* idea is to create speedily, through the intermediary of the *NFI*, an effective layer of enterprise management. Shares in each of the state firms to be privatized in this programme are to be distributed as follows: 33 per cent to a "lead" *NFI* which will then take special responsibility for that enterprise; 27 per cent to be allocated among remaining *NFIs*; 10 per cent for employees; 30 per cent for the state treasury, to be used later for a variety of purposes such as reprivatization bonds, a fund to pay for public sector wage increases, to support state pensions and perhaps simply to be in due course sold off.

10 According to the official data in 1993 the private sector accounted for 37.4 per cent of industrial sales, 84.0 per cent of construction activity and 45.2 per cent of transport services. The private sector accounted for 58.9 per cent of (end year) employment and probably for more than half of GDP produced (in 1992 its share was 47.2 per cent). A measure of the economic distance travelled since 1989 is that in that year the private sector was responsible for only 30.1 per cent of GDP and 44.3 per cent of employment. Of course, private sector predominance in employment terms is due to the structure of Polish agriculture where around 3.7 million people are engaged, 95 per cent privately. Outside agriculture the private sector share in employment declines to less than half of the total (43.0 per cent) and is, as might be expected greatest in trade (93.5 per cent) followed by construction (74.8 per cent) and 26.7 per cent in transport which of course is dominated by the large public utilities - especially the railway system. All data from *Mały Rocznik Statystyczny 1994*, (GUS, Warsaw), p. 319-20.

11 The nine were: *Bank Gdańsk SA; Bank Przemysłowo-Handlowy SA* (Krakow) privatized in December 1994; *Bank Śląski SA* (Katowice)

privatized amid a political row in February 1994; *Bank Zachodni SA* (Wroclaw); *Pomorski Bank Kreytowy SA* (Szczecin); *Wielkopolski Bank Kredytowy SA* (Poznan) the first major state bank to be privatized in 1993; *Bank Kredytowo-Depozytowy SA* (Lublin); *Powszechny Bank Kredytowy SA* (Warsaw) and *Powszechny Bank Gospodarczy SA* (Lodz).

12 See *Transforming the Polish Economy II*, (1994), where the authors note "the NBP has a considerable say in the process of transformation of the Polish economy which from a centrally managed economy has turned into a market economy. In the opinion of many Polish economists the NBP is gradually acquiring practice in performing the typical functions of a central bank in a market economy." p. 312.

13 Personal communication.

14 Such, at any rate, was the view of the Warsaw representative of the IMF, Mr Markus Rodlauer, in the summer of 1994. Interview with author.

15 The former Soviet Union was Poland's major trading partner in the planning period. In the mid 1980s (1986) it accounted for 33 per cent of Polish imports and 28 per cent of exports. By 1993 those trade shares had slumped to 9.1 per cent and 7.6 per cent respectively. A united Germany became almost the mirror image of the former USSR in terms of its importance to Poland as a trading partner: in 1993 it took 36.3 per cent of Polish exports and supplied 28 per cent of imports. It is interesting to note that in 1929 Germany was Poland's number one trading partner accounting for 31.2 per cent of exports and 27.3 per cent of imports, *Handel Zagraniczny 1992* (GUS, Warsaw, 1992, p.2).

16 The election of September 1993 divided the Polish party political scene into two: those who got into parliament (mainly the post-communist left) and those who did not (mainly the post-Solidarity right). Though well over 20 national political parties entered the September contest only six won parliamentary representation and the post-Communist parties, the Peasant PSL and the urban SLD, achieved a decisive victory. With just under 36 per cent of the popular vote the two secured, thanks to a new electoral mechanics, 66 per cent of parliamentary seats (303 out of 460 in all). The leading opposition party in parliament is the centre-left post-Solidarity UD. The political right did badly in the election securing parliamentary representation only through the KPN and the presidential party, the BBWR. On the post-Solidarity left the UP party benefited from the shift in voter sentiment and although not

formally part of the PSL-SLD coalition the UP contributed the minister of industry and tended to vote with the government on most issues. The fact that the governing coalition represented a minority (35.8 per cent) of voters is, in wider terms, not unusual: many electoral systems generate governments which command minority public support. What is however striking about the September 1993 election is that the "wasted" votes (35.4 per cent of the total) were cast mainly for right wing post-Solidarity parties. Those parties paid a heavy penalty for refusing to form strategic alliances before the September poll. Thus the Polish party political scene from September 1993 was composed of a left wing dominated parliament with the right pushed out to inhabit extra-parliamentary space.

17 The OPZZ was established in the early Jaruzelski period, in December 1984, as the "official", that is to say, communist party backed, trades union organization.

References

Gronicki, M., and Wyznikiewicz, B., (1994), *Koniunktura gospodarcza w Polsce w trzecim Kwartałe oraz prognoza na czwarty kwartał 1994 roku i pierwszy kwartał 1995 roku*, (The economic situation in Poland in the third quarter with forecasts for the fourth quarter and the first quarter of 1995), GIME, Warsaw, 26 October 1994.

Kowalik, T., "The great transformation and privatization: three years of Polish experience" in *The New Great Transformation?*, Bryant, C.G.A and Mokrzycki, E., (eds) Routledge, 1994.

Poznański, K., (1993), "Poland's Transition to Capitalism: Shock and Therapy", in *Stabilization and Privatization in Poland: An Economic Evaluation of the Shock Therapy Programme*, (Kluwer).

Rosati, D.K., (1991a), "Poland: systemic reforms and economic policy in the 1980s" in Blazyca, G. and Rapacki, R. (eds), *Poland into the 1990s: Economy and Society in Transition*, Pinter Publishers, London, p.30.

Rosati, D.K., (1991b), "The Polish Road to Capitalism: A Critical Appraisal of the Balcerowicz Plan", *Thames Papers in Political Economy*, New Series, No.2, Spring, (Thames Polytechnic, now University of Greenwich, London).

Sachs, J. (1993), *Poland's Jump to the Market Economy*, (MIT Press).

Transforming the Polish Economy II, (1994), Warsaw School of Economics.

3 Forecasting the Polish economy

Mirosław Gronicki and Bohdan Wyżnikiewicz

Introduction

Official Polish national accounting statistics have been published since the early 1960s. Until 1990 the Central Statistical Office (*Główny Urząd Statystyczny - GUS*) compiled data according to the Material Product System (MPS) concept, a UN accepted national accounting procedure, but one used exclusively by the centrally planned economies of Central and Eastern Europe and a few developing countries. The crucial weakness of the MPS was its definition of productive activity as being limited to the so called "material production sphere" which covered primary sectors, manufacturing, construction, trade and transport. This meant that the MPS system measured only a part of economic activity. Services were almost completely overlooked.

From 1987 GUS supplemented the MPS data with an annual series compiled according to the System of National Accounts (SNA), the standard UN approach to national economic accounting. This series has a starting point in the year 1980. But these data were derived from MPS categories and methodology (the old activity classifications and terminology were maintained) and this meant that the scope and quality of statistical data were not satisfactory for the creation of a national accounting system genuinely of a Western standard.

Important changes in statistical policy took place in the early 1990s when reforms aimed at transforming the Polish economy into a market system were seriously initiated. First, with the help of Western experts GUS gradually substituted the SNA for the MPS. Second, GUS, together with its research centre (*Zakład Badań Statystyczno-Ekonomicznych - ZBSE*) published an experimental set of accounts for the institutional sectors[1] covering 1991 and 1992 (Polish National Accounts, [1994]).

It was thought that new methods of national accounting would throw light on the question - what really did happen to the Polish economy between 1989 and 1991. This has been discussed by many analysts. Some expressed doubts concerning the reported level of GDP in 1989, believing that it overestimated actual conditions in the highly disequilibrated economy. Some pointed to a further statistical "overestimation" with regard to the subsequent contraction in output, investment and consumption in the following years, especially in 1990. Gomułka, for example, (1993) has insisted that GUS used a mistaken methodology in estimating price indices and that enterprise sector[2] gains from capital appreciation were incorrectly estimated.

Indeed, taking into account the very high inflation rate (244 per cent) in 1989, the disruption of the planning system, the stocks hoarded by state enterprises and the general confusion on the eve of the "big bang" in January 1990, the highly imperfect statistical system could not successfully face the challenge of the new situation.

In our opinion, official estimates of Polish GDP were unreliable in certain areas. At first, in 1990 and 1991 private sector activity and Polish imports seemed to be underestimated. Capital gains have been a controversial issue since data were first published for 1989 and 1990. Later, in 1992 and 1993 a huge discrepancy between the foreign trade data reported by GUS and the foreign payments statistics collected by the National Bank of Poland (NBP) created doubts as to the reliability of both data sets. This discrepancy is significant and amounted to 3 per cent of GDP: if one uses the NBP payments data as a guide to trade flows then GUS's estimate of GDP growth should be 3 per cent higher.

Doubts over official estimates of Polish GDP and the difficulties this created for short-run macroeconomic analysis stimulated Gdańsk Institute research into national accounting methodology and its applications to the Polish situation. A project aimed at generating quarterly estimates and growth forecasts for Polish GDP was launched in July 1993. The initial team of two senior researchers and two assistants has grown with a further six researchers in post by the end of 1994. The project is supported by the Polish-German Co-operation Foundation (using counterpart funds from the debt relief package) and the project partner on the German side is the leading economic research institution, DIW, which specialises in the analysis of the business cycle and in economic forecasting.

In the section that follows we describe the objectives of the Gdańsk Institute project. It outlines the methodology used and discusses our initial attempt to model and predict the Polish business cycle.

Objectives of the project

The reconstruction of a market economy in Poland requires the creation of independent institutions which deal with the analysis of macroeconomic development. Before 1990 government or state agencies fully monopolized the field of macroeconomic research and were the source of all professional information on the economic situation. As a result public opinion on the macroeconomic situation was informed only by official institutions.

This situation had two important shortcomings. First, it was biased by official optimism. Second, due to the lack of appropriate professional tools the information provided was one-sided: it concerned only the supply side of the economy. The latter deficiency is, in our view, more important and dangerous than the former.

Public opinion in Poland has for decades been accustomed to viewing macroeconomic developments from the perspective of the dynamic of industrial production. After 1990, inflation and unemployment rates were used as additional indicators. Then academic centres began to supplement these sources of information with survey research on business optimism. While the latter represents real progress in assessing economic conditions it has also strengthened the traditional pre-eminence of the supply-side approach in almost all economic discussion.

The available national accounts data, a natural synthetic source of information on the economic situation, could not play a useful role in economic debate because the data were published with a lag of ten or more months. The only early data usually published by GUS are provisional growth rates for a few key variables (GDP, consumption, investment, industrial production) and as such are an inadequate base for a more complete analysis of the economic situation. The Polish statistical office does not yet publish quarterly or biannual estimates of GDP.

The intention of the Gdańsk Institute's macroeconomic team was to create a tool that would deliver a quick, complex and consistent set of macroeconomic information allowing a better assessment of current economic developments and an immediate analysis of the business cycle. The only tool that takes into account aggregate supply, aggregate demand and income is an integrated set of properly constructed national accounts.

The main objective of the project was thus to provide Polish and international public opinion with an independent, regular and reliable flow of information on quarterly macroeconomic developments as well as a short-term forecast based on quarterly national accounts[3]. The prerequisite in all of this is the creation of a consistent framework for national accounts both on an annual and quarterly basis. This, in turn, requires the collection of the appropriate statistical data for estimates of quarterly GDP and its components.

An outline of the Gdańsk Institute's approach

General remarks

During the first year of project implementation we concentrated on the following areas:

1   data collection;
2   initial data analysis;
3   constructing quarterly estimates of Polish GDP.

Data collection

In the project we used a range of official sources, mostly published by government agencies as well as some auxiliary publications necessary to fill gaps in official statistics. The most important sources we made use of are shown below:

monthly Bulletin of Polish Statistics, GUS;
the NBP Bulletin, (National Bank of Poland);
the NBP's decade reports;
GUS press communiques;
annual statistical yearbooks, GUS;
GUS irregular publications such as reports on the labour market, investment, small business, foreign trade, GDP;
ministry of finance reports on the consolidated state and government budget;
Warsaw School of Economics reports on the business cycle;
foreign reports on Polish foreign trade and balance of payments

(IMF, Eurostat and DIW statistics).

An outline of the DIW approach

In this project we decided to adapt the procedures developed by DIW. The Berlin Institute has extensive experience in estimating German GDP. In fact, it was the institution which initiatied such research in Germany. Since 1989 the DIW also developed a framework for estimating GDP in the territory of what was East Germany. The point of departure for estimates and forecasts of the German economy is the general situation in the world economy, especially in the United States. The six areas shown below are the main focus of research and each is carefully monitored by one or more experts:

    consumption;
    investment;
    international trade;
    public finance;
    labour market;
    money and credit.

Researchers maintain close working contacts in order to ensure consistency, that accounts are balanced and relevant information exchanged. The work proceeds in two stages. The first step is a comparison of certain variables which should maintain elementary internal consistency with others. Take, for example, value added in construction alongside investments in buildings. In a closed economy with a one-year construction cycle the value of investment in residential and non-residential sectors should equal value added in construction. The second step is creation of a system of six accounts for four sectors of the economy, namely:

    private households;
    government;
    enterprises;
    the rest of the world.

The remaining two accounts are for the entire economy and for the Gross National Product. In each account the revenue side equals the expenditure side and most account items have to have their exact correspondent record in one or more other accounts of the system.

Unlike the first step, this set of accounts requires full consistency of records. The accounts create a closed system where the residual (solution) is the balance of payment with the rest of the world.

The DIW seperates out its historic estimates of GDP for recent quarters from its forecasting exercise. Its quarterly estimates of GDP are published before those of the official Federal Statistical Office (one to two months after the quarter). Annual GDP growth is forecast at two half year periods. Forecasts are released as the common opinion of 6 leading German economic institutes twice a year: in early May and late October. The former forecast looks ahead to the end of the current year, while the latter goes up to the end of the following year. DIW's own forecast is announced in early January and late June. Although estimated quarterly, only results aggregated to a half year forecast are made available to the public. The DIW's procedures may be summarized as follows:

GDP estimates are considered from three angles: from the production side, as a product of labour volume and productivity changes; by type of expenditure; from the income side; and made internally consistent through the four sector accounts of households, government, enterprises and the foreign sector;

econometric models and methods are applied with caution and are considered to be auxilliary tools for checking the consistency of a system. Empirical ratios, simple time trends, graphical presentations often prove useful;

variables that are correlated or somehow associated with aggregated key national accounts data are compiled in a system of working tables. In addition to statistics other relevant information is collected (for example data on mortgages, consumers, climate);

certain variables called "leading indicators" are selected. Changes in these variables are believed to indicate future changes in the GDP or its crucial components;

seasonal adjustments are applied using DIW's own methodology, the so called "Berlin method". All quarterly or six-months data are seasonally adjusted;

GDP growth rates and components are compared with the corresponding quarter of a previous year, rather than with the previous quarter of the same year;

the focus is on real changes, nominal changes are derived via price deflators;

wherever it is possible, the double-accounting rule is applied while checking out the accounts consistency each new piece of information leads to a current forecast updating.

Data analysis

In Poland we have produced, so far, the following three categories of data:

quarterly estimates of historical annual national accounts;
estimates for recent quarters that are not covered by official national accounts;
estimates for current and future quarters.

The general rule in the project is to utilise wherever possible official national accounts data. So far, we have broken this rule only twice. First, we use only one general category of gross domestic product instead of the two used by GUS. We do not make use of "Gross Domestic Product utilized" which differs from GDP by net exports. Second, we have adjusted GDP in current and constant prices for 1990 (GUS used that year as a base for producing estimates in constant prices but the official data have a discrepancy between constant and current price series). These two adjustments are in line with general SNA practice, while GUS still resorts to an MPS type approach.

In the first stage of the project we expended a significant effort on making annual series consistent and conformable to international standards. Our spreadsheet files contain both original official and transformed series. The latter are reconstructed to be consistent with the SNA (for example, we had to calculate factor incomes ourselves as the data were not readily available). Whenever new data are published the spreadsheet is updated and the transformation programme re-run.

We work on two independent quarterly accounts: GDP by expenditure and GDP by source of income. The two accounts are then balanced and reconciled. The income account plays a secondary role since the unknown residual reaches 30 to 40 per cent of GDP. GUS data on income as reported in the Monthly Statistical Bulletin cover only

60 per cent of households while information on corporate income is not reliable. The expenditure account is more accurate than the income account. The point of departure is an estimate of private consumption, government consumption and investment outlays. Historical data were used to build a macroeconomic model for forecasting two quarters ahead.

Evaluation of the Polish business cycle

In 1994, some five years after the launch of the transformation process, over 50 per cent of GDP originated in the private sector. The share of the public sector has gradually diminished but it still has a significant impact on macroeconomic developments. The rudiments of a "mixed-economy" with strong market mechanisms have already been established and the first signs of typically market economy behaviour of economic aggregates - including a business cycle - have been observed.

The Polish business cycle is just emerging. After the stabilization programme of 1990 and the "transformation recession", the Polish economy started to grow in 1992, a growth fuelled by factors typical in the market economy. Below we present our view of the Polish business cycle. But it should be remembered that the research continues and the results are not final.

To evaluate the Polish business cycle we used the DIW methodology, adopted and adjusted by the Gdańsk Institute macroeconomic team to fit Polish circumstances. This generated quarterly GDP series starting from the first quarter of 1990 with, at the time of writing, estimates for the third quarter of 1994. Some results are presented in Figures 3.1, 3.2 and 3.3.

The results of our analysis were published in quarterly Gdańsk Institute reports on the performance of the Polish economy. The first report was published on 17 January 1994. In each report we present our estimates of Polish GDP by quarters, ending on the previous quarter with forecasts for two consecutive quarters. Reports are usually published four weeks from the day the quarter ended.

The GDP series may be used in macroeconomic analysis of Polish economic growth. So far, our interest focussed on the following questions:

1   the take-off point, when did the Polish economy stop contracting?;
2   what was the impact of various government decisions on economic performance? (we were especially interested in the impact of the

special border tax[4] introduced in December 1992 and VAT introduced in July 1993);
3   what are the major sources of growth in Poland?;
4   what are the major obstacles to growth?

Our analysis suggests that the stabilization programme of 1990 had a strong influence on the Polish economy in the first half of 1990. All macroeconomic aggregates were affected. Domestic demand contracted strongly, as expected, and the undervalued Polish złoty, and reform of Polish trade, helped in generating a significant growth in net exports. However, the level of net exports in the first quarter of 1990 was quite small; it started to increase more rapidly in the following quarters. In the second half of 1990, domestic demand rebounded strongly and the GDP level in the fourth quarter was in fact the highest for 1990. It is difficult to explain why this happened. We believe that a mixture of factors was responsible: rather strong consumption demand, growing exports and mistaken expectations in the state-owned enterprises resulted in increased inventories of unwanted production. Inventories increased also in the first quarter of 1990 but this was simply due to an abrupt contraction of domestic demand.

The economy slowed again in 1991. This time responsibility lay with a combination of contraction in demand by firms and a fall in exports (a fixed exchange rate regime combined with very high inflation led to a real złoty appreciation). There was no offsetting influence from private or government consumption.

In the second half of 1992 the economy started growing. The major source of growth was domestic consumption and exports. Domestic demand was additionally pushed up by the expectation that a special import tax of 6 per cent (on top of existing tariffs) would be introduced from January 1993. This small increase in import costs caused frantic buying in the fourth quarter of 1992 and had spill-over effects in stronger private consumption and investment demand.

This was quite unlike what happened in the first half of 1993 and especially in the second quarter of that year. Expectations of higher prices for many goods and especially imported goods, prompted a large increase in domestic demand. Our estimate shows an annual increase of private consumption in the first and second quarters of 7 and 8 per cent respectively. The surge in domestic demand meant that in the second quarter of 1993 GDP grew by around 8 per cent. This high growth rate depleted inventories which were only slightly rebuilt in consecutive quarters.

The strong domestic impulse became slowly exhausted in the third and fourth quarters of 1993. GDP growth rates fell to 3 or 4 per cent. The slowdown coincided with the world economy moving out of the recession. Polish exports growth started to accelerate. Foreign demand translated into a higher than expected growth rate of manufacturing output. The GDP growth rate went up again. In the third quarter of 1994, it was 6 per cent and was expected to reach 4-5 per cent in the two consecutive quarters. Domestic demand was, however, sluggish. A low rate of growth of real income of households (1-2 per cent) is responsible for the poor performance of sectors other than manufacturing. The summer drought in 1994 negatively affected agricultural output. Divergent growth rates in sectors have also some impact on domestic demand. Investment was growing but not in the most efficient sectors. Residential investment was declining and the number of housing completions in 1994 was the lowest in the post-war period.

Manufacturing is the only fast growing sector. Is it possible that it will maintain a high growth rate in 1995 and 1996? Our analysis, presented in our October 1994 report (see *Gronicki and Wyżnikiewicz 1994*), suggests that foreign demand will slow in the second half of 1995 and demand for the Polish goods will slow even earlier. Due to Poland's uncompetitive export structure, and with EU barriers to trade, Polish exports will grow less rapidly and as results the rate of growth of Polish industry will also slow. Without significant new sources of domestic demand we expect that Polish GDP growth may decline.

This simple macroeconomic analysis examines only some aspects of the Polish business cycle. We have not discussed monetary and fiscal policy here since the former is unsophisticated and concentrates (with mixed results) on fighting inflation and the latter is practically non-existent.

Figure 3.1

GDP, industry and construction

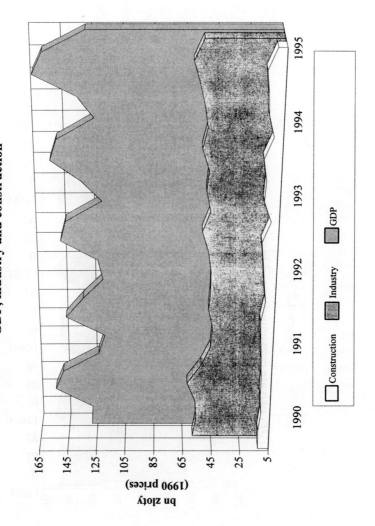

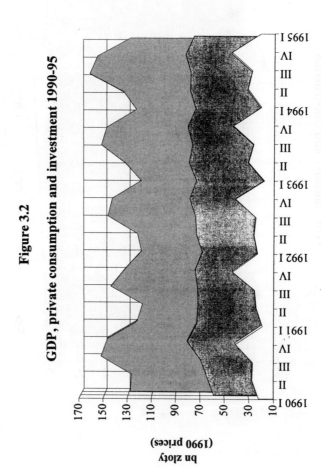

Figure 3.2

GDP, private consumption and investment 1990-95

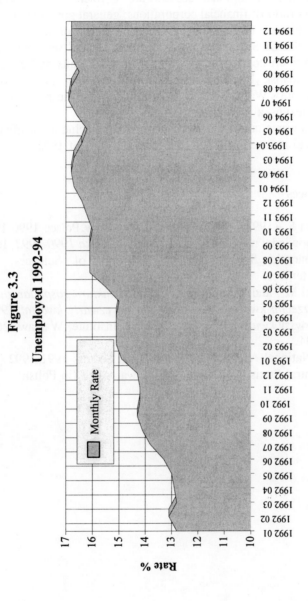

Figure 3.3

Unemployed 1992-94

Monthly Rate

Rate %

1992 01	
1992 02	
1992 03	
1992 04	
1992 05	
1992 06	
1992 07	
1992 08	
1992 09	
1992 10	
1992 11	
1992 12	
1993 01	
1993 02	
1993 03	
1993 04	
1993 05	
1993 06	
1993 07	
1993 08	
1993 09	
1993 10	
1993 11	
1993 12	
1994 01	
1994 02	
1994 03	
1993.04	
1994 05	
1994 06	
1994 07	
1994 08	
1994 09	
1994 10	
1994 11	
1994 12	

Notes

1 The six institutional sectors are defined to be: non-financial corporations; financial corporations; general government; non profit institutions; households and the rest of the world.

2 For the GUS definition of "enterprise sector" see note 1 p.35.

3 The interested reader may obtain further details of the regular flow of Gdańsk Institute forecasts by contacting the authors at the Institute's Warsaw office, Instytut Badań nad Gospodarką Rynkową, Sapiezyńska 3, Warsaw, 00-215, Poland.

4 This was a tax of 6 per cent on imports (including tariffs already in place) reduced to 5 per cent from the start of 1995.

References

Gomułka S. (1993), "Polityka stabilizacyjna w Polsce 1990-1993: odpowiedzi na pytania", *Gospodarka Polska 1990-1993*, Institute of Economic Science, Polish Academy of Sciences, Warsaw, September.

Gronicki M., and Wyżnikiewicz B., *Koniunktura gospodarcza w Polsce w trzecim kwartał oraz prognoza na czwarty kwartał 1994 roku i pierwszy kwartał 1995 roku*, Gdańsk Institute, Warsaw, 26 October 1994.

Polish National Accounts by Institutional Sectors 1991-1992 (1994), Central Statistical Office, Warszawa, April (in Polish).

4 State-owned enterprises under pressure

Janusz M. Dąbrowski

On the threshold of systemic changes in the Polish economy at the end of 1989, the public sector accounted for 82 per cent of GDP, for 67 per cent of total employment (87 per cent excluding agriculture) and managed more than 8,000 enterprises. From then, as a result of transformation processes, the role of the public sector in GDP generation and in employment declined substantially. At the end of 1993, the public sector accounted for only some 40 per cent of national economy employment (54 per cent of employment outside agriculture) and its share in GDP fell below 50 per cent. The number of state-owned enterprises fell to 6,000 (since 1991 the rate of decline in their number slowed considerably because larger entities have been split into smaller ones). This dramatic change in economic proportions was attributable on the one hand to a "shrinkage" of the state-owned sector, where adjustment and in some cases plant closure led to a drop in employment, and on the other hand to the dynamic development of the private sector. Almost 1,000 state-owned firms were privatized by the end of 1993 with another 2,000 enterprises involved in the process of ownership transformation.

Despite the marked decline in the significance of the public sector in the Polish economy in the 1990s one must not overlook the fact that the success of the reform process and indeed the condition of the entire economy still depended in a decisive way on that sector. In accordance with the philosophy of the transformation programme it was hoped that the tough macroeconomic policy being pursued would intensify the adjustment activity of all economic agents, including state-owned enterprises. This was of great significance since the systematic process of public sector privatization would, it was assumed, take at least one decade (Balcerowicz, 1990).

In this context, it seems important to consider to what extent the implementation of a new economic policy based on hardening the budget constraint for enterprises (the control of cash inflow, real positive interest rates, wage-growth control) as well as radical institutional changes found their reflection in the way state-owned firms adjusted to new economic conditions. Where adjustments take place was it effective and did it allow enterprises to meet the needs of the developing market environment? It is also useful to try to identify barriers and problems that emerged in the course of transformation and it is important to examine the social dynamic of restructuring within the firm. Differences between enterprises in terms of size, market position or industry sector turned out to be important determinants of enterprise responses to new conditions.

Political and social conditions underlying macroeconomic policy

Since its start, the state of economic transformation in Poland was determined by two equally significant factors. First, macroeconomic policy clearly had an impact. But second, the adjustment measures undertaken within the firm, by economic agents, were critical. This included the responses of enterprises from the former public sector, as well as both "old" and "new" private firms. From the beginning of 1990 when the so-called Balcerowicz programme was first implemented, until the parliamentary elections of September 1993, economic policy consistently pursued a clearly specified direction, despite various competing opinions and recurrent political pressures aimed at its revision. This direction was fixed on a firm anti-inflation priority alongside steps to open the economy internationally together with a strong commitment to sweeping institutional and ownership changes (especially privatization). The relative uniformity of the set of economic instruments applied, which gave the economic transformation process credibility and provided a bench mark for the creation of new social attitudes, was also important. These new social attitudes crystallized both among those who saw, and still see, the new reality as a chance for themselves - the new entrepreneurs - as well as among those who were more defensive or even hostile to change.

The former, although relativity strong in numbers, were from the very beginning scattered and seemed disinterested in lobbying in support of market reforms. On the other hand the emergence and consolidation of movements which resulted from social and political frustration was a potential threat to the transformation programme. Tensions reached a climax in the parliamentary elections of September 1993. The crushing defeat by post-communism of parties originally responsible for systemic reform revealed the scale of popular disappointment with the effects of the transformation and the longing for the relatively safe existence under the "paternalistic" socialist system.

Mounting social and political resistance to the reform process has, since 1991, led to a slow-down in the pace of change. It seems that the turning point was the presidential campaign of late 1990, when the reform direction was officially and publicly challenged and exceedingly high social expectations were created. General election campaigns (in the autumn of 1991 and 1993) and government crises (the collapse of the Olszewski government in June 1992 and the vote of no confidence in the Suchocka government in May 1993) led to the consolidation of a block whose interests lay in slowing down the reform process if not challenging its very foundations. While in the early stage of reform the OPZZ (the trade union organization created by the communist authorities in the 1980s) was "dormant" and "Solidarity" supported change, later, the radicalism of demands put forward by the trade unions started to grow. At the same time political parties and social organizations increasingly encouraged their rank and file to challenge the reform process. Programmes were built around slogans that challenged the sense of existing economic policy. Social acceptance of the effects of economic transformations also diminished as high expectations became frustrated.

Fortunately, the social and political situation was, and still is, more complex and paradoxical that a simple reading of trade union and political programmes, and even public opinion polls, might suggest. Trades unions and political parties in opposition to Solidarity governments busied themselves by drawing up programmes built on the basis of social discontent (substantially instigating this discontent), challenging the reform programme (slowing down its implementation) and political radicalism (from extreme nationalism through de-communization of the state to visions of civilized socialism). The paradox of this situation lies in the fact that the post-communist parties which took power in September 1993 were relatively quick to abandon their pre-election pledges, and follow, with only minor modification, the existing thrust of the transformation. Society on many occasions expressed its conviction in the necessity of reform while at the same time voicing dissatisfaction over the impact of these changes. This was frequently noted in public opinion surveys (see for example, CBOS, Dąbrowski, 1992, 1993a, Kloc and Rychlowski, 1994). All of this means that the threats to the reform process in Poland are considerably less serious than one might expect if political and trade union declarations and random public opinion polls are taken at face value. The challenge to transformation is rather to be found at the level of discourse; it is, fortunately, not translated into effective action.

The adjustment measures undertaken by all economic agents, especially enterprises, are the second, significant factor influencing the state of the economy under transformation. The depth and scope of the enterprise's responses are decided by features related to its environment, the enterprise's standing at the outset of market reforms, as well as the attitudes and skills of its internal leaders. Gdańsk institute research shows that firms tended to adjust more speedily and more easily the more intense the negative signals (such as the competition getting tough, the decline in demand for the firm's products or loss of selling outlets) reaching the concern from its environment.

It should also be stressed that the former private sector found it easier to adjust to the new market rules of the game although even this adjustment was not completely smooth. Private firms were better acquainted with operating without the protective umbrella of the state. They faced more difficult starting conditions and tougher competition. Their relatively small size may also have been an advantage. The problems faced by the public sector were certainly more acute from the very beginning of the transformation process. Lack of preparation for functioning in market economy conditions was in many cases reflected in helplessness, a wait-and-see attitude, and an unwillingness to take action in view of uncertain outcomes. Virtually all firms faced adjustment problems but the slowest ones to adapt to the changed environment were large, and very large, state-owned enterprises and former monopolists.

State enterprise responses

The adjustment reactions of state-owned enterprises were slower and more shallow than the authors of the reform programme expected. These expectations were based on an assumption that the re-emerging market would force intensive adjustment activities on all economic agents. This however was not the case for at least two reasons. First, changes in the regulatory framework were incomplete. These changes were designed to put market economy principles into motion, to restrict firms' access to easy money (abolishing subsidies, allowances and payments deferrals possibilities) and, by the same token, they also aimed to attach real value and real meaning to economic categories. But "easy money" (Kornai's notorious soft budget constraint) was quickly replaced by mounting payments arrears and "paper money" (amounts registered but very difficult to make a use of). This of course made accounting for actual profits and losses extremely difficult (for further details see Calvo and Corricelli). The mainly state-owned enterprises making chronic losses, which in the past had enjoyed large scale state support and protection (subsidies), started to base their economic existence on rapidly growing debts (not meeting their obligations) to efficient firms and banks. In this way, the chance of eliminating the permanent loss-makers, responsible for the quick rise in payments arrears, was considerably reduced. The situation was also made difficult by the uncertain fate of many creditors, threatened by the bankruptcy of their debtors. The scale of this phenomenon was reflected in the growing share of loss-making firms in the total number of state-owned enterprises, from 20 per cent in 1990 to more than 40 per cent in 1993 ("*Sytnacja Społeczno Rzeczpospolita*", 1991, 1994).

It should, however, be noted that at the end of 1989 and in the first quarter of 1990 state-owned enterprises achieved an artificially high level of average profitability. Profitability, defined as gross profits to total costs, reached almost 40 per cent. This high profitability of enterprises on the threshold of systemic changes resulted, first of all, from the very high rate of inflation which accelerated to over 800 per cent in 1989 and was greater than 150 per cent in the first quarter of 1990. Enterprises purchased raw materials and semi-products at prices much lower than those at which they sold finished products, and the difference was entered in the books as the enterprise's profit. At the beginning of 1990 profitability was also influenced by the decline in the proportion of net labour costs in the value of turnover due to the imposition in January 1990 of a wage growth tax: at the end of 1989 this share was some 12 per cent, while in January 1990 it fell to only 7 per cent (Wyżnikiewicz, 1990). Moreover, for firms with a considerable share of convertible-currency exports in total sales, the one-off devaluation (by 30 per cent) of the Polish złoty against the US dollar in January 1990 was an important factor generating extraordinary profits.

The transformation programme was less radical in its microeconomic reform than it was on the macroeconomic level. Tough rules leading to the permanent closure of loss-making state-owned enterprises were not implemented. Closures were delayed because of cumbersome, lengthy and ineffective bankruptcy procedures. At the very outset of the transformation it was decided not to close large enterprises since these were strongholds of powerful trade union organizations. Consequently, despite the launch, by the end of 1993, of liquidation proceedings against more than 1,000 state firms, the chance was lost to acclimatise firms quickly to new market economy conditions, and, with the passage of time, this turned out to be increasingly difficult to achieve. The opportunity was also lost of avoiding, or at least diminishing, the bad debt and inter-company payment arrears problem. This strangled cash flows and the effective allocation of resources throughout the entire economy.

It took public firms rather a long time to come to terms with the new reality. Their adjustment activities were mostly of an "extensive" nature, using up reserves accumulated in the past. The process of learning about market realities did not advance quickly, especially due to shortcomings in management thinking and skills. Firms' adjustment efforts concentrated mainly on organizational changes, product adjustments not involving investment outlays, and, finding new sales possibilities. Among other things, these measures involved employment shedding, laying off part-time staff and peasant-workers, early retirement schemes, cuts in production of goods difficult to sell, cheap modernization of production, upgrading the quality of goods, more attention to packaging, more aggressive selling behaviour and flexibility in price setting. Deeper changes or preparation and implementation of restructuring programmes were rare in 1990-91.

The first firms to react to the new environment were those facing the toughest competition. They tended to be producers of consumer goods and services. Theirs was the earliest and most painful confrontation with the demand barrier. Their lack of response in the first half of 1990 caused immediate difficulties with sales and, consequently, rapidly mounting financial problems. This was noticeable among enterprises operating in light industry, food-processing and electronics, where production in the first year of the transformation fell by some 20 to 40 per cent (*"Sytnacja Społeczno Rzeczpospolita"*, 1991).

Monopolists and suppliers of raw materials and semi-products were much slower to respond to the new situation. In many instances, it was only the second wave of the transformation shock, with the collapse of exports to the former CMEA countries in early 1991, that forced adjustment processes within these firms. Growing import competition created a completely new situation for former domestic monopolists and was also an important stimulator of change. These firms lacked experience and managerial know-how. The problem of inherited bad habits and managements' shortcomings was much more acute here. This was made worse by the shortage of finance to support more deeply rooted development programmes.

After almost four years of transformation as markets became more uniformly competitive this factor began to have less and less impact on the intensity of adjustments in state-owned enterprises. First, the number of industries and firms operating in a comfortable situation with no competition fell dramatically as a result both of the dynamic development of domestic small business and the rise in import competition. Second, "tight" money, the demand barrier and competition changed the mentality of those who until recently used to dictate market conditions.

While over time the pressure of competition was systematically becoming less important in prompting state firm adjustment strategies, firm *size* was consistently an extremely important feature. From the very beginning of the transformation medium-sized enterprises enjoyed the most favourable circumstances. Their situation at the starting point was better than that of both large and small enterprises (see Table 4.1). The dynamic of profitability in medium sized firms over the whole four-year period was comparable to that of small firms. But small firms faced some disadvantages. They usually had no established links with foreign firms, nor any developed distribution network nor highly skilled staff. All these were reserved in the old system for large enterprises which enjoyed a privileged position in the economy. This is why we should stress here the dynamic efforts of small firms to find new selling outlets in Poland as well as to enter foreign markets. Over 1990-93 small firms increased the share of exports in their sales from 18 to 22 per cent, while in medium-sized companies this figure dropped from 24 to 22 per cent and in large enterprises from 26 to 15 per cent (see Dąbrowski et al 1993a).

Table 4.1
Profitability and enterprise size*
a - first half year;   b - second half year

Firms	1990		1991		1992		1993	
	a	b	a	b	a	b	a	b
Small	25.9	22.7	14.1	7.6	6.4	5.1	5.2	5.4
Medium	36.2	33.1	16.3	15.0	7.5	6.6	7.5	7.6
Large	25.0	14.3	-3.6	-25.0	-24.4	-40.2	-34.5	-34.5
Total	30.0	25.0	10.2	1.9	-1.7	-6.9	-5.0	-4.7

*   For the purpose of this paper we define a small firm to have up to 500 workers, with medium-sized firms employing between 501 and 2,000 people and large ones more than 2,000. This division illustrates much better the actual differentiation of Polish firms than that traditionally used in writings on this topic (up to 200, 200 to 500, above 500), due to the considerable concentration of capital, the result of developing industrial giants and mono centrism in state investment policy - and the high degree of monopolization of centrally planned economies. Profitability is defined as the ratio of gross profits to total costs.

Source: Dąbrowski et al (1993a)

Small firms were also active in adjusting their product ranges. They were the first to attempt to modernize production, to make quality upgrades and even to launch new products. Changes in employment and wage structures were also deepest in small and medium-sized enterprises. They were usually implemented in the first two years of the transformation as part of a conscious adjustment programme accepted by the main actors within the enterprise. In large firms such adjustments happened much later, usually forced by the appalling financial condition of the enterprise.

Large and very large state-owned enterprises have been a major problem area since the very beginning of transformation. The scale of their difficulties is largely attributable to the relatively small adjustments they made. They were also poorly prepared for operation in market conditions. Their managements were accustomed to privileges in competing for state funds and they were used too to forms of political protection. All of this meant that these enterprises were the hardest-hit by systemic changes. Many directors viewed the launch of the stabilization programme as yet another attempt by the authorities to stimulate only some moderate efficiency-oriented changes at the firm level. Therefore, in 1990 most of them chose a (non-adjustment) strategy of waiting until the changes (presumed to be short-lived) were over. When it turned out that the reform was being implemented with unusual determination and, indeed, was irreversible, many enterprises embarked on hasty attempts at survival strategies. Unfortunately, by 1991 and 1992 most simple reserves within firms were exhausted and any market advantages enjoyed in the late 1980s became irrelevant. Despite the ever more apparent need for substantial adjustment radical solutions were rarely selected. Usually, under strong pressure from trades unions and employees' councils, these enterprises aimed to maintain the status quo for as long as possible. Changes in employment, wages and internal organizational structures were limited. New products, or attempts to enter new markets, were rare. The internal power structure, with very strong employee representation, was undoubtedly the major factor hampering change.

Large enterprises were not only enclaves of weak and inconsistent internal adjustments but also centres of loss-making activities. Most of them were loss-making for a long time with little chance of finding a way out of their difficult financial position. Only a few, thanks to particularly dynamic managements and the acceptance of changes by employees, were able to maintain their market position and preserve an economic existence. Worse still, large, loss-making enterprises were "a black hole" absorbing funds and creating mounting payments arrears. They then became a potential source of serious social conflict with the rise, due to inevitable closures, of unemployment. Because of their political significance governments took only sporadic and half-hearted steps to close them.

The structure of payment arrears in the public sector clearly indicates that since the beginning of the transformation process small and medium size enterprise were the informal source of credits for most large firms (see Table 4.2 and Figure 4.1). Generally, firms with higher than average profitability supported loss-making enterprises. This came about because of the inter firm relationships that existed. It was the result of fixed co-operation and technological links among enterprises and the maintenance of sales alongside deferred, and sometimes irretrievably lost, payments. It was only from 1992 that creditors started to take a tougher stance towards debtors. This, in turn, was prompted by mounting financial difficulties in the entire enterprise sector. Many firms set up special debt recovery departments, hired specialized firms to take care of debt or directed cases to the courts. Unfortunately, the effects of these measures were relatively modest.

Table 4.2
Receivables to payables ratio (end of the period)

a - first half year;   b - second half year

Firms	1990		1991		1992		1993	
	a	b	a	b	a	b	a	b
Small	1.4	1.3	1.1	1.4	1.3	1.2	1.1	1.1
Medium	1.6	1.7	1.8	1.9	1.7	1.4	1.4	1.3
Large	1.0	1.0	0.9	0.8	0.7	0.5	0.4	0.4
Total	1.4	1.4	1.4	1.5	1.3	1.1	1.0	1.0

Source: Dąbrowski et al (1993a)

Figure 4.1
Enterprises receivables to payables ratio by profitability

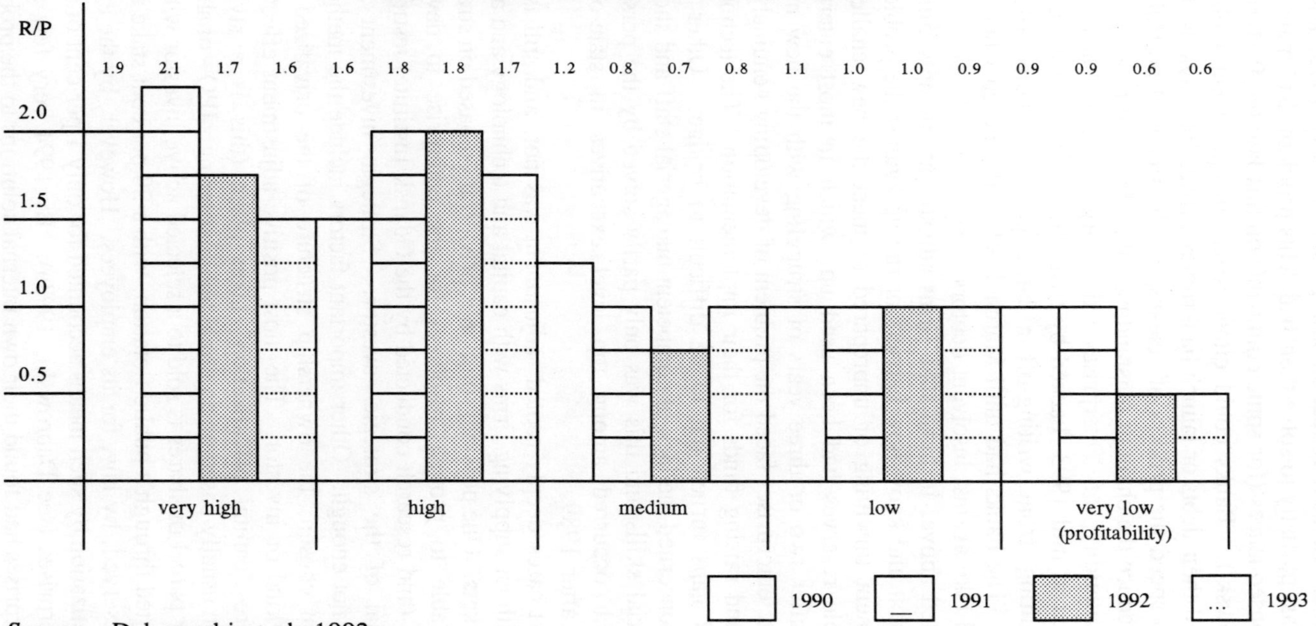

Source: Dąbrowski et al, 1993a

-- 63 --

The so-called debt reduction law passed in early 1993, allowing banks at least partially to solve their bad debts problem, had many more positive consequences (for some comments on this law see Parfiniewicz and Żebrowski). Banks could either reach an agreement with their debtors, sell their debts or launch bankruptcy proceedings against firms. In order to speed the process of "cleansing" the financial portfolios of banks, to reduce the chain of outstanding obligations and to improve the financial liquidity of enterprises, the largest state banks were recapitalized in mid 1993, backed by treasury bonds to cover possible losses resulting from writing-off a large part of credits lost (see Gomułka). The banks had until March 1994 to decide on what action they would take against insolvent debtors.

As noted above, in most state firms adjustment attempts stumbled on investment and know-how barriers or ran up against the problem of a management unwilling or unprepared to meet the new challenges. After simple reserves had been used up, which in most enterprises happened after two or three years of struggling with the new market reality, state enterprises faced the problem of developing genuinely new strategies and raising funds for their implementation. The technology and capital gaps turned out to be difficult to bridge. Other acute problems concerned the lack of competent managerial staff and shortage of managerial skills and this was only partly solved by the personnel shifts which occurred among top level executives in state-owned enterprises after 1989.

In most cases deeply rooted adjustment was not, and still is not, possible without supplying firms with capital and technology and access to new markets. One possible solution is privatization based on strategic investors, able to provide resources for the enterprise to develop. Experience (and research conducted by the Gdańsk Institute) testifies to the potential of the strategic investor. Strategic investment alone however is not enough. Other important factors include the method of privatization chosen, the ownership structure of the privatized firm and/or the kind of investor. The most positive adjustment effects are found where "capital privatization" takes place (this is a style of privatization usually based on an initial public offering - IPO - of shares) and a major parcel of shares is sold to a selected active investor with the rest distributed through a public flotation, with a 20 per cent stake in the company reserved, by law, for its employees. However, by the end of 1993, privatization by such means accounted for only 1 per cent of state-owned enterprises (see Dąbrowski, 1993a). By 1994 very few state-owned enterprises had found their own internal solutions to the problems they faced, few had managed to come to terms with the new market conditions and were able to develop without substantial external support.

The structure of power in state owned enterprise

The attitudes of the main actors in state-owned enterprises, including the enterprise director, the president (and often members) of the employee council and trade union leaders, were considerably differentiated in the transformation period. It its first stage, for several months in 1990, there was a dominant disbelief in the firmness of the new economic policy line. Later, from the second half of 1990, this was replaced by a more active phase when some deliberate preparation to meet change took place. The next stage brought a fear of the new reality and some attempt seriously to look for survival strategies, to start more or less complex adjustment and sometimes also restructuring measures.

The power structure in the state firm, often viewed as unclear yet with a strong determination to block radical change, was of much significance. Decision-making powers and responsibility is scattered among management, the employee council and the trades unions. This set up is the result of the "self-managing" nature of state-owned enterprises as guaranteed by the important 1981 law defining the nature of the state firm. That law gave state-owned firms decision-making sovereignty, a limited financial independence and the opportunity for the employee council to participate in shaping enterprise activities. Among other things, the council had the right to appoint and dismiss the enterprise director, it had to approve the annual balance sheet and profits distribution and set the directions of the firm's development. It also had the power of veto over privatization plans. The employees' council's broad range of powers flowed from a strong Polish tradition of self-government consolidated through numerous failed attempts to reform the centrally-planned economy. But is was also down to the fact that the self-management lobby was particularly influential in the period when the state enterprise bill was drafted in 1980-81.

Trades unions are the other crucial element in the power structure. Their strength became apparent only after Solidarity was re-legalized and an open internal struggle began for influence over state-owned enterprises. This involved the post-communist OPZZ union, Solidarity, and many other unions, most of them of only local significance, which emerged after 1989. Although with no formal place in enterprise government the unions participate in key decision making. They have an impact on personnel, strategic and privatization issues. They are often strong, with considerable employee support: the extent of unionization ranges from 40 per cent of the workforce in small firms to more than 70 per cent in large ones (see Dąbrowski et al, 1992). They often have the power to stage protest and strike actions going beyond a single enterprise. Moreover, the leaders of enterprise-level trade union organizations are often engaged in political activity: OPZZ activists are closely connected with the post-communist left (indeed it has MPs in the parliament elected in September 1993); the Solidarity trade union is associated with centre or right-wing parties and other unions with both the extreme left and right. These political connections add a new dimension to potential conflict within an enterprise.

Some analysts claim that the enterprise director is the weakest link in the power structure. Although this thesis cannot be generalized for the whole spectrum of enterprises, one may suggest that the director's position weakens with enterprise size. In small and medium-sized firms, especially those performing well, directors usually enjoy a strong position, even being "protected" from employee discontent by employee councils, and (though less frequently) by trades unions. This "non-aggression pact" arises when labour leaders are convinced of the need for radical action and so support the director. In this, for the director, comfortable situation, management may behave autocratically trying to limit, if possible, the influence of the employee council and trades unions on operational and strategic decisions.

In large enterprises, the director's position is weaker due to the strength of powerful trade union organizations, the potential for protest action, the political aspects of conflicts and the ambitions of labour leaders, many of whom in the early 1990s were themselves appointed as directors or embarked on political careers. In such conditions managing the enterprise becomes an arena for permanent compromise and painstaking negotiation. In many cases, this leads to overt conflict, a conflict rooted in the poor economic position of the enterprise. Quite often, a radical rescue package and restructuring programme, with far-reaching concessions on the part of employees, is the only way. However the work force rarely accepts such solutions and will often try to transfer the conflict to a higher plane, making it a dispute with government, aiming to win access to special allowances, subsidies or debt forgiveness, or pressing for the dismissal or resignation of management.

However, this apparently messy tripartite power structure need not always lead to negative outcomes. In the early stage of systemic change this same structure stimulated reform-oriented programmes in many firms which were being run in a conservative and inefficient way. At that time, employee councils and Solidarity performed a crucial role in inspiring change, especially in view of the passive attitude taken by a major part of so-called *nomenklatura* management (that is, those appointed in the previous periods mainly because of political loyalty to the communist party). Sometimes this constellation of forces offered enterprise directors employee support for more decisive actions. On other occasions it prompted the dismissal of management which was unable to make radical decisions. Interestingly, there were only rare cases of naked political retaliation against managers. Directors were rarely removed when no better candidates existed although in 1990-91 around 50 per cent of managers were dismissed and replaced with new appointees. The latter were usually younger, better educated, and more dynamic than their predecessors, and were often nominated from among the enterprise employees: in many cases they were employee councils' leaders or middle ranking executives (see Dąbrowski et al, 1992).

One should also mention in this context the coalitions formed in the most active firms between directors and Solidarity dominated employee councils, or between directors and the Solidarity union, even against the will of a majority of employees. The initiative for such co-operation would often come from enterprise directors keen to introduce radical changes and seeking strategic support from those groups representing employees. Such directors usually enjoyed a good name among the trade union decision-making bodies and the employee council members. They were able to demonstrate their flexibility, competence, and ability to anticipate coming developments. In many cases these directors had prepared for the transformation process long before the stabilization programme was implemented.

Over time, Solidarity support for radical internal changes in state-owned enterprises clearly waned. It seems that mid-1991 was a turning point after which Solidarity became less reform-oriented and more "demands-oriented". This process tracked the growing social dissatisfaction with the reform process. It also shadowed the more active stance taken by the OPZZ and other unions (especially Solidarity-80) whose far-reaching demands gradually succeeded in crowding out Solidarity from enterprises. With politicians, intellectuals and advisors leaving Solidarity and joining political parties and ruling cabinets, the trade union decided to take a sharp turn and become a demand-voicing employee organization. This meant challenging the direction and pace of the transformation process. It meant arguing more strongly for the protection of social benefits and for softer monetary and tax policies including the removal of the *popiwek* tax on excess wages growth[2]. It meant pushing for a slow down in the pace of privatization. Undoubtedly this undermined the broad reform coalition and made enterprise-level adjustment more difficult.

As trades unions became more aggressively "demands-oriented" directors often approached the employee councils for support. The councils began to take upon themselves the role of mediator and became a means of calming the mood in state-owned firms. But the councils were also seen both by management and employees as a new interest group, one less and less representing employee interests, but also not particularly concerned to strengthen the position of enterprise directors. As the councils attempted to stabilize the situation in the firm they tried to win more control over the strategic decisions facing the enterprise. A (usually) fragile consent in favour of continuing the reform programme at the micro level could be achieved but only at the price of its dilution.

Generally speaking, while in 1989-90 the structure of power in state-owned enterprises contributed to, or at least did not impede, necessary and favourable internal changes in the firm, in the later period it became an increasingly strong barrier to restructuring programmes or active adjustment measures.

Tensions and conflicts

In the early period from 1990 enterprise level tensions and conflicts were not deep or protracted enough to become an organized permanent protest against transformation leading to its marked dilution or even rejection. Moreover, enterprise level conflicts, developing into protests and strikes, were not always signals that internal change was being resisted. Especially in the early stage of reform, employee pressure was often aimed at *initiating* active enterprise adjustment, or at least at formulating a plan to save the firm from collapse when market competition became severe. Employees often tried to force conservative enterprise managements to revise their approach and, whenever mild forms of persuasion failed, changes in management were enforced by means of protest actions and strikes.

From the point of view of social peace, the first two years of transformation in 1990-91, were extremely calm in the state firm. In 1990 only 250 strikes were registered. In 1991 this increased but only to 305. This relative tranquillity was sandwiched between much more intense strike activity in 1989, with almost 900 strikes, and 1992 and 1993 when it accelerated to considerably more than 6,000 per annum (*Rocznik Statystyczny*, 1994). The relative calm of 1990-91 was due to the very high level of social optimism in the early stage of the transformation process backed of course by Solidarity support for the reform process.

Generally, there was a logical development with regard to tensions or conflicts in state-owned firms throughout the transformation period. In 1989-90, they were concentrated, first of all, on personnel shifts among the *nomenklatura* enterprise managements with most change at that time at managing director or middle-management levels. Next, the conflicts of 1990 and 1991 concerned mostly wage issues, focusing on the fall in real wages, the impact of the wage-growth tax, the *popiwek*, and on redundancies. Employee protests were directed "outwards" against a government policy which limited public sector wage growth but they also had an internal dimension which concentrated on the scale and pace of cuts in employment. Following a period in which lay-offs were accepted, especially regarding part-time and unproductive workers, labour organizations began to view the matter more aggressively. Where firms were in deep financial trouble, with radical action the only way of staving off bankruptcy workers usually agreed to a limited number of redundancies.

From 1992, privatization became an important focus of disputes at the enterprise level. These usually concerned, and still concern, the new ownership structure of the enterprise (who will hold the majority share?), the matter of selling to foreign investors or distribution of shares among the insiders. Sometimes, this conflict was played out between the enterprise and the ministry of privatization or the firm's "founding body"[3], while on other occasions it was a conflict inside the firm, a struggle of interest groups looking for the best, from their point of view, method of privatization. In many cases, the conflict was sparked by fears of job insecurity or of strengthened work discipline.

Irrespective of protests fuelled by enterprise restructuring, throughout the entire transformation period there were various strikes against the deteriorating financial situation employees in some public sector industries or in the budget-financed sphere found themselves in. There were, for example, strikes of miners, steel workers, textile industry workers, railway workers (several times), teachers and doctors. Protests fuelled by discontent with the effects of reforms were first observed at the end of 1990 and then re-appeared every few months in the following years. They usually subsided for several months when a new government was formed only to return with double intensity when it turned out that the economic situation of a given group did not improve and perhaps even deteriorated. It was only the Suchocka government which came to power in July 1992 that had the misfortune to face *immediately* a massive strike, the expression of protest against the incessant financial deterioration of state-owned enterprises, the decline of real wages in the budget-financed sector, and, at the same time, a signal of social disapproval of the bitter confrontation that had just been played out between the government, parliament and president during May and June 1992, the latter an internecine conflict difficult to understand for an average observer of the political scene (see Kloc, 1992).

It is worth noting, however, that the growing number of strikes in 1992 and 1993 was coupled with a decline in employee support for this kind of action. The number of those who believed that a general strike was inevitable also fell from some 70 per cent of employees in 1990 to 42 per cent in 1993 (see Gardawski). Moreover, those with a good job and wage appeared less and less willing to support and be identified with trade union protests or with those struggling for better pay or for jobs. The possibility of a mass protest against transformation seems to diminish with the overall improvement in the economic situation and the progress of public sector privatization[4].

Summary

Four years of economic and systemic transformation certainly reveal a falling support for the reform process and this has affected the pace of change although without altering its direction or nature. Under the new more demanding conditions imposed by a market environment the private sector operated more efficiently and dynamically. State-owned enterprises needed more time to come to terms with the new situation and where adjustments took place they were smaller than expected or needed.

Enterprise adjustments in the state sector involved, firstly, simple measures carried over from the previous period (laying off effectively redundant workers, reduction of inventories, cuts in materials and energy costs, stripping unnecessary assets). More active adjustment, going beyond this ran into capital and technology barriers. An unclear structure of power in the state-owned enterprise also created difficulties as did the poor preparation of internal actors to meet the restructuring challenge.

Nevertheless the changed and more demanding economic environment forced state-owned enterprises to take steps to adjust to market requirements. This was an organizational and functional shock for many firms. Most state-owned enterprise experienced a cut in employment, simplification and change of the organizational structure, re-modelling of the motivation system including a linking of wages to results alongside cuts in social allowances. Changes were also introduced in sales policy including a search for new markets, price reductions, discounts, and sales promotion involving the setting up of marketing departments, participation in fairs, and general advertising. As enterprises became more responsive to market needs so production patterns started to change. The manufacture of "failed" products was largely discontinued, the output assortment was diversified and the quality of products upgraded. However, the depth of many of these actions was limited by the scarcity of capital for investment. There were only rare cases of expansion into new (especially foreign) markets, or of new product launches. Adjustment strategies also quickly hit other barriers such as the managerial (lack of competent leadership) and the organizational (dilution of responsibility for the decision-making process). Unfortunately, for many state-owned enterprises the only chance of survival lies in very intensive qualitative changes. This usually means the need to enter into strategic alliances and privatization.

It should also be noted that the situation across public sector firms was considerably differentiated in the 1990-94 period. The transformation shock was relatively well tolerated by small and medium-sized enterprises while the economic condition of large and very large firms clearly deteriorated. The latter had been operating in comfortable conditions in the central planning era, with ample subsidies and special allowances, and were completely unprepared for operation under changed conditions. Over time, they became a threat to the transformation programme, as their responsiveness to change was, and still is, the smallest. This was due to organizational and functional maladjustment as well as strong employee opposition to change. Apart from that they also became "black holes" in the system of mutual financing between firms that soon appeared. These firms were usually indebted to the budget (taxes were simply not paid), to banks (the source of bad debts) and to other enterprises. Furthermore, the scale of their indebtedness increased from one period to the next, adding to the difficulties encountered by creditor firms. The implementation of the debt reduction programme, covering enterprises and banks, only partly solves the bad debt problem, as the main culprits are the permanently loss-making economic giants for which there is no room in the market economy and which should be either completely restructured or simply closed. This, however, requires a great deal of political will, sizable funds and social consensus.

In the light of these observations it would be wrong to suggest that the only reason for weak and surface adjustments of the public sector was associated with trade unions and employee councils although this may be true for some groups of large enterprises. In the first period, both Solidarity and many councils played a positive role in stimulating adjustment measures with the barrier to adaptation often found to lie with conservative firm management. In the latter period, with a large part of enterprise management replaced by new blood, with the OPZZ intensifying its demands and Solidarity simply withdrawing its support for the reform process, the employee councils took over the role of mediator in the enterprise power structure. The cases where the trades unions or councils deliberately "petrified" inefficient enterprise structure were, however, relatively rare.

Certainly, adjustment was weakened by the situation in some state enterprises where the responsibility for decision-making was scattered and compromise solutions were sought. On the other hand, and in other cases, it facilitated the "peaceful" implementation of change, allowing social tensions to be diffused within the enterprises and not "on the street" where they might so easily have become uncontrolled. This is especially important in Poland with its strong and active employee organizations and relatively weak and scattered institutions promoting the rights of employers.

In this context, the dissipation and fragility of the political arena, which throughout the four democracy building years failed to provide a stable foundation for systemic changes, was also significant. The volatility and complexity of the political scene, coupled with the constant struggle of minor parties for voters, led to the emergence of economic programmes capitalizing on frustration, disappointment and fear, while generating great hopes and unjustified social expectations. The lack of consolidation of a strong political movement around the economic transformation programme was one of the major causes of the fundamental shift in the political arena in autumn 1993 when the post-communist coalition swept to victory in parliamentary elections. Fortunately, this radical political change does not seem to be jeopardizing the transformation process. Shortly after taking power the coalition shed its populistic election slogans and continued the economic reform programme in a form which does not differ much from the programme of its predecessors.

Notes

1   This section is based largely on Gdańsk Institute research, see for example, Dąbrowski et. al., 1991, 1992, 1993a.

2   The *popiwek* was introduced as a critical anchor of the macroeconomic stabilization policy implemented from January 1990. Price liberalization was bound to generate demands for wages compensation, and, to avoid a new prices-wages spiral, the authorities declared that permissable average wages growth would be linked to prices via a coefficient determined in advance. In the first phase of stabilization this coefficient was set at 0.6. If enterprises granted wage awards beyond this threshold a punitive and steeply progressive tax regime was applied. The *popiwek* was a source of much trade union criticism in the later part of the transformation period and was due to be withdrawn by the end of 1994.

3   The founding body is the ultimate owner of the enterprise and often represents a range of state interests drawn from the central adminstration (mainly ministries and regional authorities - voivoidships).

4   In privatized enterprises the average level of unionization and the scale of discontent is considerably lower than in the public sector (see Dąbrowski et al, 1993a).

References

Balcerowicz, L. (1990), "Budujemy społeczeństwo ludzi zaradnych" (We are building an economy of capable people), speech to parliament, reported in *Rzeczpospolita*, April 7.

Calvo, G.A., and Corricelli, F., (1993), "Inter-enterprise arrears in economies in transition", paper presented at the conference *Output Decline in Eastern Europe: Prospects for Recovery?*, IIASA Laxenburg, November.

CBOS, Komunikat z badań, (1994), (Communique of the public opinion poll centre), Centrum Badania Opinii Społecznej, (CBOS, March).

Dąbrowski, J.M., Federowicz, M., and Levitas, A., (1991), "Polish State Enterprises and the Properties of Performance - Stabilization, Marketization, Privatization", *Politics & Society*, No.4.

Dąbrowski, J.M., Federowicz, M., and Levitas, A., (1992), "Przedsiębiorstwa państwowe w drugim roku transformacji gospodarczej", *Transformacji Gospodarki*, No. 27, Gdańsk Institute for Market Economics (GIME).

Dąbrowski, J.M., Federowicz, M., and Levitas, A., (1993a), "The State-owned Enterprises in the Process of Economic Transformation: 1992-93", *Economic Transformation*, No. 38, (GIME).

Dąbrowski, J.M., Federowicz, M., Kaminski, T., Szomburg, J., (1993b), "Privatization of Polish State-owned Enterprises: Progress, Barriers, Initial Effects", *Economic Transformation*, No. 33, (GIME).

Dąbrowski, J.M., (1992), "Parlamentarzyści o prywatyzacji", (Members of parliament on privatization), *Rzeczpospolita*, September, 10.

Dąbrowski, J.M., (1993), "Prywatyzacja kapitalowa", (The "capital" path of privatization", *Życie Gospodarcze*, No.22.

Gardawski, J., (1994), "Robotnicy 1993. Wybory ekonomiczne i polityczne", (Workers 1993. Economic and political choices), Ministerstwo Pracy i Spraw Socjalnych, (Ministry of Labour and Social Affairs), Warsaw.

Gomułka, S., (1993), "The Financial Situation of Polish Enterprises 1992-1993 and its Impact on Monetary and Fiscal Policies", paper presented at the conference *Output Decline in Eastern Europe: Prospects for Recovery?*, IIASA Laxenburg, November.

Kloc, K., (1992), "Inny Sierpeń", (A different August), *Przegląd Społeczny*, No. 5.

Kloc, K., and Rychlowski, W., (1994), "Strajki w polskim przemysle. Wnioski z badań", (Strikes in Polish Industry. Research findings), Warsaw School of Economics, mimeo.

Parfiniewicz, A. and Żebrowski, J., (1993), *Restrukturyzacja finansowa przedsiębiorstw i banków. Ustawa z komentarzem*, (The financial restructuring of banks and enterprises. The law with commentary), Centrum Informacji Menedzerow, (Management Information Centre), Warsaw.

Pinto B., Belka, M., Krajewska, A., Krajewska, S., Sierhej, R., (1992), *Transforming State Enterprises in Poland: Microeconomic Evidence on Adjustment*, World Bank - Polish Mission, mimeo.

Rocznik Statystyczny 1994, (GUS, Warszawa, 1994).

"Sytuacja społeczno-gospodarcza w 1990r", (1991), *Rzeczpospolita*, February, 7.

"Sytuacja społeczno-gospodarcza w 1993r", (1994), *Rzeczpospolita*, February, 7.

Program gospodarczy: Główne założenia i kierunki, (1990), (The economic programme: Main assumptions and directions), (The council of Ministers, Warsaw).

Wyżnikiewicz, B., (1990), "Sruba", (Wage pressure), *Gazeta Bankowa*, No. 45.22.

5 The political constraints on Polish privatization

Jan Szomburg

Over the course of the last five years of economic transformation (1990-94) the share of the private sector in Polish GDP has grown from 10 per cent to more than 50 per cent. In 1994 more than 60 per cent of the work force was employed in the private sector. This private sector growth is the result of both the state's sale or leasing of assets ("top-down" privatization) as well as the creation of new private firms ("bottom-up" privatization). Within the framework of top-down privatization some 300 enterprises have been sold to private investors over the course of the last five years. Another 800 have been leased and about 1000 have had their assets sold off following their legal liquidation as state enterprises.

The denationalization of state firms in 1981

In Poland, the decisive step towards denationalization was taken in 1981. At the time, the 10 million-member Solidarity movement forced the communist authorities to pass legislation which gave state firm managers and democratically elected employee councils wide ranging decision making powers. Indeed, one can say that central planning in Poland came to an end with the passage of this legislation, and that enterprises became - at least formally - fully independent entities with respect to their productive and investment activities.[1] The control of firms' assets, in short, was from that point in time located within firms themselves.

The "insiders", or stakeholders, acquired a wide range of property rights but these were neither exclusive nor transferable.

Throughout the 1980s however the autonomous decision making powers of managers, and employee councils were constrained by, on the one hand, the logic of an economy of shortage, and, on the other, by the direct influence (through *nomenklatura* personnel policy) of the communist party on managers. Nonetheless the councils continued to function throughout the decade. In 1989, when the regime finally collapsed, and before new political parties had emerged from within Solidarity, the councils constituted a powerful para-political social movement. Next to the rapidly fragmenting Solidarity movement, the councils were the only organized social force capable of opposing the economic strategy put forward by the Mazowiecki government. Moreover, they represented the particular interests of the insiders employed in state firms.

The dilemmas and compromises of 1990

Within the first post-communist government, that headed by Tadeusz Mazowiecki, there were two approaches to the question of state enterprise autonomy. The first assumed that privatization had to be preceded by the return to the state of real control over state firms. The advocates of this approach proposed a once for all, universal, re-nationalization of state enterprises and their legal transformation into joint-stock companies solely owned by the state treasury. This legislative act was designed to reduce the powers of insiders (managers and employee councils) granted by the 1981 law on state enterprises. The government was to acquire all rights to make decisions about when and how to privatize "its" assets and employees were to receive only certain restricted economic benefits from the process. In other words, they were to get a limited number of shares in privatized firms at preferential prices.

The second approach to privatization aimed not only to maintain enterprise autonomy but to extend it. Workers' councils were to be given complete control over managerial selection and state firms were to be granted greater control over their assets, including the right to sell-off parts of them, and to veto privatization plans proposed by the state.

In practice, the second approach won out. The decisive factor in this victory was the fear that a new field of social conflict would open up within firms at the same time as the Balcerowicz plan radically reduced inflation, output, and real wages. There was also a desire to decentralize economic responsibility and this prompted a greater respect for the autonomous decision-making powers of enterprises and generated a wide ranging authority on the part of workers' councils. In short, insiders - workers, managers and the council - became responsible for the economic and financial health of their firms, a responsibility that would have become less well identified with re-nationalization.

Thus, in 1990, the state gave insiders both *de jure* and *de facto* control over enterprise assets. Only if firms broke the law, failed to pay taxes, or operated at a loss was the state empowered to intervene in their operation. Similarly, insiders acquired not only the possibility of receiving preferential treatment during privatization, but were granted decision making powers over the process as a whole. The legislation on privatization gave employee councils and managers the right to initiate privatization procedures, as well as the right, at least temporarily, to block privatization plans coming from the state. At the same time however, the council of ministers and the prime minister, retained the power to begin privatization procedures against the will of firms on a case by case basis.

The negotiated character of Polish privatization in 1991-93

Those responsible for privatization within the central state only reluctantly accepted the compromise embedded in the legislation passed during 1990. In practice however, the state's power vis-a-vis insiders steadily weakened in the following years. Indeed, it proved practically impossible to privatize state enterprises against the will of employee councils and managers, despite the legal possibility of so doing.

Meanwhile the political fragmentation that accompanied the creation of a new democratic regime made it difficult for parliament to arrive at any sort of strategic consensus with respect to privatization. Unable to arrive at such a consensus within the state and for the country as whole, a series of weak governments was forced to pursue privatization on a case by case basis. Indeed, the inability to reach a consensus at the national level compelled the government to look for consensus at the micro level, firm by firm.

In mid 1992 a wave of strikes organized by the trade unions threatened the stability of the Suchocka government (the fourth Solidarity administration formed since 1989) and led state officials to propose the creation of a so called "enterprise pact". Among other things, this pact increased the negotiated nature of Polish privatization by enhancing and formalizing the role of the trade unions in the process (the key case motivating this formalization was that of the Gorażdze cement works where the trade unions had effectively blocked the government's efforts to sell the firm to a foreign investor).[2] As such, the Polish state remains only a nominal owner and cannot presently privatize its assets according to its own will. Instead, it is forced in each case to negotiate the acceptance of a particular privatization procedure with insiders: trade unions, employee councils and management.

The political weakness of the government and the attempt to achieve a working consensus

The activities of all Poland's post-Solidarity governments were constrained by the specific workings of a highly fragmented political arena and by the logic of a political market in which there is a surfeit of small and fiercely competitive factions. Privatization, in fact, is one of the most instrumentalized issues in the political game. The inability to achieve a consensus with respect to privatization in parliament forced the government to make all sort of concessions to individual firms. In practice this means on the one hand that privatization has not produced serious conflict between the government and the collective mass of insiders. On the other hand, however, it has slowed the pace of privatization while simultaneously compromising its economic character through endless, and not necessarily rational, negotiations. At the same time, Polish society began to suffer from what has been called "transition fatigue" and the overall support for reform declined.

This was the situation the Suchocka government found itself in when it proposed that an "enterprise pact" be drawn up with the trades unions. The idea was that in order to get the social support necessary radically to accelerate the privatization process the government had to give more economic privileges to workers (20 per cent of shares allocated free of any charge), draw them into the process as a whole, and grant them a permanent place on the corporate boards of privatized enterprises. The pact was accepted by the national organs of the trades unions and was debated in the Sejm throughout 1993. It requires enterprises, or more exactly, the factory committees of the trade unions, to propose their own privatization plans within six months. If they fail to do so, all decision making powers with respect to privatization revert to the state. The pact was therefore an attempt to accelerate privatization by making it possible for the state eventually to take back control over "its" enterprises. It was an attempt to win continued popular support for reform, and in particular for privatization by moving towards a model of social corporatism. In the end, however, for the Suchocka government, the effort failed. In May 1993, before parliament could pass the enterprise pact legislation, the Solidarity trade union initiated, and won, a vote of no confidence against the Suchocka administration, despite the fact that Solidarity was to be the main potential beneficiary of the pact itself.

The pact was a product of the Suchocka government's inability to achieve a consensus on privatization within parliament. Indeed, the government suspected all along that even if it achieved such a parliamentary consensus, it would not do much to alter the real situation within firms. In fact, the government decided that parliament was a much less important partner with respect to privatization than the trade unions. But this approach was always likely to have its costs: the economic quality of privatization was likely to be endangered. In thousands of enterprises property rights would indeed become both exclusive and transferable. At the same time however, the ownership of these rights would become hugely diffuse and would emerge only at the expense of both foreign and domestic strategic investors.

Thus, as the general election of September 1993 approached, privatization in Poland remained trapped in something of a vicious circle. An open but still infant political market was a powerful source of uncertainty and instability. The best possible remedy for this uncertainty was and is quick and far reaching privatization. And yet the speed of privatization remained constrained by the same political struggles that it would ultimately resolve.

The vote of no confidence and the fall of the Suchocka government had far reaching consequences. New parliamentary election were held in September 1993, elections which proved disastrous for all political parties that had emerged from the Solidarity movement. Indeed, the trade union itself lost all its representatives in the lower house. Meanwhile two-thirds of all seats were won by the two post-communist parties - the urban Democratic Left Alliance (SLD) and the rural Peasants' Party (PSL). A coalition government was formed under premier Waldemar Pawlak (PSL) which managed to hold together throughout 1994 and survived into 1995.

In this way, four years of "liberal revolution" in Poland came to an end and the September election showed that society had ceased to tolerate the liberal medicines for the sickness left by communism. The people let it be known that they were both tired of reform and nostalgic for more stable and less challenging times, nostalgic for the welfare state that they had grown accustomed to over 40 years of communist rule.

The vote of no-confidence initiated by the representatives of the Solidarity trade union was an early expression of this change of mood, an expression of the inevitable disappointment of the people with respect to their own revolution, its results, and their leaders. The political fruits of this disappointment were harvested by the post-communist parties with their naturally *etatist* outlook, a fact which had obvious consequences for the actual pursuit of privatization in Poland. Before looking at their policies however, it is worth summing up the gains, losses and institutional conditions which governed the privatization policies of the post-Solidarity governments in the four years immediately following the collapse of communism. These governments were, in general, of a liberal orientation and all saw privatization as a priority within the larger efforts to transform the polity as a whole.

Weak government and autonomous state enterprises: pluses and minuses 1989-93

The *de jure* and *de facto* autonomy of state enterprises has, however, had its advantages. Above all it made possible a wide variety of informal privatizations which were very important for the growth of the new private sector. The first wave of informal privatization began in 1987-89, during the last years of the communist regime. This was driven by new legislation that made it easier to establish private businesses. Overnight, tens of thousands of new private enterprises sprung up around state firms, enterprises which were owned and/or controlled by the managers of the firms they surrounded. These managers then diverted state firms' revenues, assets, know-how, skilled labour and market contacts to their new private concerns. They did this in a variety of ways, but as one might suspect, ways that disadvantaged the state sector. Nonetheless, this parasitical feasting on the state sector laid the foundations for the rapid growth of an important segment of the private sector. This was *nomenklatura* privatization where the main beneficiaries came from the ranks of the old party apparat.

The conditions for informal privatizations improved after the political breakthrough of 1989 as the decision making powers of insiders increased. It is worth noting in this context that in 1990 firms became the legal owners of their buildings and land, broadening the range of assets that came into informal play. The leading role in these informal privatizations was again played by managers. In all probability some several hundred enterprises were purposely brought to bankruptcy by their managers. Before these firms collapsed, however, managers transferred income to new entities and then purchased on the cheap whatever remained of value within the "mother" enterprise. The spectacular effects of *nomenklatura* privatization in turn sparked the ownership instincts of the workers.

Thus from 1991-93 this "model" of *nomenklatura* privatization was extended to include all insiders as coalitions of managers, employee council members and workers laboured together to privatize their firms. Frequently, these coalitions conspired to divert state enterprise profits into a variety of illegal of semi legal funds. These funds were then used to help employees purchase shares in new joint stock companies, companies which in turn leased the assets of the original state enterprise from the state. In fact, this kind of practice underwrote many of the 800 leasing type privatizations noted earlier.

The Balcerowicz plan, with its elimination of shortage and its imposition of hard budget constraints, added a further impulse to privatization. Indeed, it set in motion a process which can be called "privatization through auto-consumption": as firms encountered financial difficulties they began to sell-off or lease unwanted machinery, equipment, vehicles, buildings, warehouses and land. A huge number of assets flowed from the state to the private sector in this way. Even today, a great number of enterprises exist only because the have been slowly but steadily consuming their assets. A spectacular case of this is the progressive selling off of the state owned shipping company's fleet.[3]

In sum, one can say that the *de jure* and *de facto* weakness of the state as an owner made possible the swift transfer of assets from the public to the private sector, but that this happened quite independently of the state's attempt to sell off entire firms. These informal transfers have, despite both their economic and moral costs, proved to be a more efficient way of privatising state assets than the top down methods that were pursued in formal privatization programmes. Moreover, and on the whole, they had a positive impact because the transformed assets are much better utilized now than they were before.

The weakness of the state has also had both positive and negative consequences for its *own* attempt to sell off entire state firms. On the one hand, the inability to privatize firms against the wishes of the workforce reduced social tension and conflicts. On the other hand, it slowed down the speed of formal privatization and worsened the economic quality of those privatizations that actually took place. For instance, the majority of the employee-owned enterprises that lease state assets have very diffuse and egalitarian ownership structures.

The government's weakness also delayed the preparation of plans to privatize and restructure heavy industries such as mining and metallurgy, and the country's energy and transport infrastructures. Here, powerful unions, employee councils, and managers made government officials very afraid to address these sensitive issues and distorted the economic rationality of plans that did emerge. Take, for example, mining: instead of the government's initial plan to create about 20 holding companies capable of rationalizing activity and employment an industrial concern structure will be created which is likely to be less capable of enforcing efficient adjustment within the sector.

If one considers the overall immaturity of the political system in the first four years after the fall of communism and the instability and uncertainty this created, the general balance of pluses and minuses resulting from the weakness of the government's ownership position must be considered positively. The wide stream of spontaneous, informal transformations of state assets has made possible the quick growth of the private sector. The restructuring of heavy industry, while still difficult, is now easier than it was because many of the sector's assets have already been transformed. Moreover, the private sector is now able to absorb greater numbers of the unemployed.

Privatization and the rebirth of "state capitalism"

From the moment that the post-communist parties formed their coalition government in late 1993 a change in the overall course of economic policy could be observed: preference for a liberal model of a market-based capitalism was replaced by a model of state capitalism.

This change meant that the primary goal of the Pawlak government was no-longer the privatization of state enterprises but the "rationalization of their management". Indeed, the central idea governing the coalition's legislative initiatives with respect to state enterprises was to improve the state's control over them by reducing the scope of their independence. The government therefore proposed the mass "commercialization" of state enterprises, or in other words their wholesale transformation into joint-stock or limited liability companies owned by the state treasury. If their plans were achieved it was expected that some 3,500 enterprises - virtually all remaining state firms not already being transformed through other procedures would be commercialized in 1995.

The technical aspects of the Pawlak government's programme for mass commercialization represented a return to an idea considered first by the Solidarity government of Tadeusz Mazowiecki. Nonetheless, at that time, mass commercialization had a different goal: it was seen as a way to simplify and speed up privatization.

For the post-communist government, however, the same instrument was being used to serve different ends. In short, the post-communist parties wanted a return of the real direct control over the economy that they had in the past engaged and with which they were already familiar. But their desire for a more "hands on" system of enterprise control was more than simply an effort to reassert their political control over the economy. Rather it was also connected with an effort to make the wages system within the state sector more amenable to individual adjustment.

In its election campaign, the post-communist SLD promised the liquidation of the so-called *popiwek* tax on excess wage growth[4]. This tax was put in place by the ministry of finance under Balcerowicz and was designed to ensure that largely independent state enterprises did not blindly submit to the wage demands of work-forces that played strong roles in dictating enterprise strategy. The coalition government headed by prime minister Pawlak aimed to remove this much resented tax and played on the hopes of the unions that after commercialization pay would be dependent only on the will of enterprise directors.

Another new goal of commercialization was supposed to be the restructuring of state enterprises by the state within the framework of larger sectoral plans. Earlier Solidarity governments had no illusions about this sort of industrial policy and hence concentrated their efforts on privatization.

Alongside changes in the goals of commercialization there were changes in the socio-political possibilities of actually realising the policy. In short, the possibilities for actually implementing a mass commercialization programme were significantly greater in 1994-95 than they were earlier. First, the Pawlak administration was the only government since 1989 that had a clear majority in parliament. Second, despite a 5 per cent annual rate of growth of GDP created mostly by the private sector, privatization had become discredited in the eyes of the public. There was a certain nostalgia for the welfare state and for the old and known games of manipulating the state as an employer. This "escape from freedom" was not just an individual phenomenon, but one shared by the work-forces of entire factories. In this political situation, it was much easier for the government to defeat the employee councils that previously stood in the way of commercialization and which would be eliminated by it.

Nonetheless, in 1995 the battle had yet to be played out to the end. Among other things, the trades unions had not clearly stated their position on the issue. On the one hand, commercialization would facilitate their pursuit of wage gains by eliminating the excess wage tax. On the other hand, however, it would mean a loss of power within enterprises on other issues because they would lose the ability to influence employee councils and hence to hire and fire directors.

Even if mass commercialization was to be carried out in 1995, however, it is not at all clear what its impact would be. One likely negative outcome was a slowing down of the privatization of small and medium sized enterprises, the majority of which were privatized through sales to individual investors or through leasing arrangements, and not through the sale of shares. Positive effects were more dubious. The chances of improving the management of state enterprises were minimal. They had already proved that as "self-managing" firms - constrained by the tax on excess wages - they were capable of fairly extensive adjustment to the market. Their renationalization was therefore liable to do little more than facilitate wage demands vis-a-vis a state which would once again clearly become responsible for "its" enterprises. Moreover, the effort to restructure commercialized enterprises was likely to cost the state budget dearly and risked weakening, with demoralizing effect, the financial constraints on state firms.

Moreover, privatization itself looked likely be motivated solely by efforts to increase budgetary revenues and not by any larger attempt to improve the micro-economic functioning of a market economy. Even in 1994 the governing coalition stressed the importance *for the budget* of privatization and increased privatization revenues from 1.6 per cent of the total in 1993, to 2 per cent in 1994, with an expected 2.9 per cent in 1995. This rise in budgetary revenues from privatization, however, was not accompanied by any increase in the tempo of privatization measured in terms of the number of enterprises actually transformed. In fact, this tempo clearly declined in 1994 and looked likely to fall again in 1995. Nonetheless privatization revenues were expected to increase by focusing on individual enterprises in attractive sectors such as banking and tobacco.

The slowing of privatization was in line with existing social preferences: survey data showed that about 70 per cent of the population was against it. This was an expression of society's general rejection of reform - of which privatization was an important symbol - as well as society's feeling that much of what was achieved in the area of privatization was accomplished unjustly. These feelings were in large part due to the media's focus on pathological cases of privatization at the expense of showing the positive gains that privatization made possible.

The *etatist* orientation of the governing post-communist parties combined with the existing social mood could produce an attempt to build state capitalism in Poland. Such an attempt would undermine the accomplishments of the liberal Solidarity governments and would probably produce a decline in the economy's rate of growth. Over the longer term, however, such a decline would probably lead people once again to turn to the road of free market reform.

In any case, the best privatization strategy for Poland appears to be a continuation of the pluralistic one that was pursued between 1990 and 1993. Its foundation is to maintain a certain balance between the various addressees of privatization, as well as a certain plurality of forms and methods. It would however be extremely advantageous from an economic point of view if the role of both managers and domestic investors could be increased. The realization of such a strategy, however, still requires the achievement of a certain minimum political consensus in parliament, as well as the evolution of new methods of privatization and the more flexible use of existing ones.

Notes

1   With this legislation state enterprises became independent (*samodzielny*), self-managing (*samorządowy*) and self-financing (*samofinansowy*). It was known as the reform of the "three s's". For further details see George Blazyca, *Poland to the 1990s: Retreat or Reform?*, (Economist Intelligence Unit Ltd, Special Report, No. 1061, 1986), pp 24-25, pp 39-43 (eds).

2   The Gorażdze plant, the most modern cement works in Poland, built in 1977 and located in the Opole province in the south west of the country was eventually sold to the Belgian concern *Cimenteries CBR* in July 1993. A few months later the Belgian firm sold on 43 per cent of its equity to a leading German building materials producer, *Heidelberger Zement*. However in the run up to privatization CBR had to defeat a rival bid for a worker-management buy-out (eds).

3   It was possible, for example, for individuals to buy ocean going tugs in Gdańsk at bargain cash prices in 1990-91 with very little formality involved (eds).

4   See p. 72, note 2.

6 An overview of the Polish privatization process

Janusz Lewandowski

Introduction

Although privatization is a world-wide phenomenon, it acquires additional dimensions in Poland and in other post-communist countries. Dismantling the public sector is a crucial factor, but only one among the many contributing to the reconstruction of a market economy from the ruins of central planning. The institutional and behaviourial vacuum constitutes an additional barrier to privatization in central and Eastern Europe. The smooth and efficient progress of ownership transformation itself requires a market framework - that is a price mechanism, a mature financial system and capital market, legislation safeguarding property rights and contracts as well as bankruptcy procedures and standard accounting practices. That environment is nonexistent or just emerging in our countries.

Privatization in Poland is more than a way of constructing a new corporate governance structure designed to fill the gap left by the withdrawal of the state. Privatization involving capital, new technology, managerial know-how, is the most effective way of restructuring and modernising the country's obsolete industrial stock. Practically all state-owned enterprises need some form of operational or financial restructuring and, therefore, restructuring is virtually inseparable from privatization.

Practical experience shows too that privatization can be an effective way of enforcing international standards - economic as well as environmental. Strategic investors are expected to bring acquired companies up to European standards, paying clean-up costs, although a portion of costs anticipated may be deducted from the initial price of a privatized company. Hence, one other important aspect of privatization is that it is also a vehicle for the integration of the Polish economy with the developed economies of the West.

The complex task of ownership change embraces:

1 privatization of state-owned enterprises of various types and size;
2 privatization of financial institutions (banks, pension funds);
3 municipal privatization;
4 "improvement" of the property rights structure in the co-operative sector;
5 restitution of property nationalized after World War II.

Central and Eastern Europe countries share several privatization characteristics in terms of starting point, scale, typical barriers and social constraints. The state sector of course is the dominant part of the economy. In Poland, for example, in 1989 the state sector encompassed some 8,500 enterprises generating 75 per cent of GDP. It was also a heavily concentrated and monopolized sector. But superimposed on this essential layer of economic activity each country also has several distinctive features. Poland's specific traits include the following:

1 a relatively larger private business sector than typical for socialist economies. Of course, Poland's predominantly privately-owned agricultural sector was a unique phenomenon among Comecon countries. In 1989 the Polish non-farm private sector accounted for 10.3 per cent of industrial production and 14 per cent of the non-agricultural labour force;
2 the strong trade union tradition of Solidarity and a generally influential labour movement;
3 the rapid "small privatization" of some 2,500 enterprises in retail, construction and service sectors.

This paper describes the experience of four years of privatization in Poland and identifies some lessons which can be drawn from our case, perhaps, for the benefit of other countries.

The institutional framework and organization of privatization

The first schemes for large scale privatization were developed after the establishment in September 1989 of the Solidarity government led by Tadeusz Mazowiecki. At that time there was great optimism that privatization would make quick headway and be socially accepted. The newly established office of the "Plenipotentiary for Privatization" (the precursor of the privatization ministry), together with Western advisors, began preparing the legislative and institutional framework for privatization. Quite soon it became clear that the modest human and material resources allocated to the giant task of ownership transformation were totally inadequate for the task in hand and the initial optimism faded. Limited institutional support became one of the constraints in Polish privatization. By 1994 this institutional framework of ownership transformation had the following features. It included the central and local offices of the privatization ministry, the agricultural property agency, the securities commission, the state foreign investment agency and it relied on a clearer definition of the powers of the so-called "founding bodies"[1] (the owners, see below p. 89) of state firms.

The Ministry of Privatization
(Minsterstwo Przeksztatceń Własnosciowych - MPW)

The MPW was set up in August 1990 to implement and supervise the programme of property transformation in Poland. In 1994, the head office in Warsaw employed 340 people. According to the privatization law of 13 July 1990, the main duties of the ministry were defined to be:

1 preparation of government privatization policy;
2 the sale of shares or stock of state enterprises using a variety of methods;
3 development of policy regarding direct foreign investment to Poland in co-operation with the ministry of foreign economic relations (Ministerstwo Współpracy Gospodarczej z Zagranicą - MGzZ);
4 monitoring the privatization process;
5 co-operation, in matters of privatization, with trades unions and chambers of commerce;
6 professional training for management in the fields of privatization and the securities market.

The ministry thus initiates, supervises and controls the process of restructuring and privatization. It also prepares amendments to existing regulations and drafts projects for new laws in an attempt to ensure the smooth progress of ownership changes.

The regional structure of the MPW

The regional structure of the MPW was established in the second half of 1991. The scope of the regional offices' work includes the initial verification and consideration of applications for privatization and other allied projects submitted within the framework of "capital privatization" (the public flotation of state companies) and privatization through liquidation (a popular privatization route involving the sale of assets in whole or in part of liquidated enterprises). The regional offices are also charged with providing information, organising promotional features and training management with regard to privatization.

At the end of 1994 regional offices existed in Białystok, Bielsko-Biała, Kraków, Gdańsk, Katowice, Kielce, Lublin, Łódz, Poznan, Rzeszów, Szczecin, Torun and Wrocław. They co-operate with the regional authorities which act as "founding bodies" for some state firms. They also collaborate with local government which is increasingly active in the privatization of municipal enterprises. In 1994 the regional MPW offices employed 115 persons in all.

The state agricultural property agency

The agency was set up by the act on the administration of state-owned agricultural property in October 1991. The primary goal of the agency is the restructuring and privatization of state farms. Liquidated farms are disposed of by sale or lease to individuals or legal entities. Importantly, when it comes to land, the law permits agricultural property to be leased to foreign subjects only with the consent of the ministry of agriculture and foods (*Ministerstwo Rolnictwa i Gospodarki Zywnosciowej - MRiGZ*). In the case of sale of such property to foreign purchasers the consent of the interior ministry (*Ministerstwo Spraw Wewnętrznych - MSW*) must also be sought.

"Founding bodies"

The "founding body" of the state enterprise is its owner, some might say a rather "artificial owner". Typically the founding body is constituted of representatives of central ministries, directors of central institutions, the 49 regional authorities (vovoidships) and local authorities. The founding body represents the state treasury and is charged with controlling and assessing state firms' activities. The law on state-owned enterprises and the privatization law permit founding bodies to intervene in the operation of state firms.

The securities commission and stock exchange

The securities commission was set up by a new law in March 1991. This was the precursor to the establishment, after a gap of over 50 years, of the Warsaw stock exchange (*giełda*). The commission is charged with:

1   supervision of trade and competition in the public securities market;
2   organising and ensuring the efficient functioning of the securities market and the protection of investors;
3   the development of the securities market;
4   promoting the principles governing the functioning of the securities market.

The state foreign investment agency
(Panstwowa Agencja Inwestyjce Zagraniczny - PAIZ)

The state foreign investment agency was set up when in July 1991 a new law was passed on companies with foreign capital participation. It offers various forms of assistance to foreign investors (information regarding potential Polish partners and on specific sectors and regions in Poland). Its objective is to present a comprehensive service to attract foreign companies to invest in Poland although this is something increasingly taken up by regional and local authorities. It also carries out comparative analyses of foreign capital flows in Central and Eastern Europe.

Methods and scope of privatization

In September 1990, the MPW prepared its first privatization programme. It reflected an initial optimism which assumed in the 1991-95 period some 50 per cent of all state firms would be privatized. On the other hand, it recognized that, given the scale and complex nature of the challenge, any analogies to privatization in the West or in developing countries would be misleading (see Lewandowski, Szomburg [1990]). A truly innovative strategy was necessary, as reflected in the multi-track approach that actually emerged as well as the specifically Polish concept of mass privatization. It soon also became apparent that the Polish privatization programme, based on a bottom-up philosophy and heavily decentralized, could not set precise quantity targets for privatization. In Poland the broad thrust of privatization, including more precise objectives for disposal of state assets, are set by parliamentary decision voted on as a supplement to the annual budget. The overall result is that a privatization "map", and associated "map" of branches excluded from privatization, is gradually emerging through sectoral studies and practical experience. This reflects the relatively decentralized model of Polish socialism, allowing for the substantial autonomy of state owned firms before 1989. Poland and Hungary were, in this respect, different from other communist countries (especially East Germany and Czechoslovakia).

With the exception of the defence industry, no one particular sector of the Polish economy has been explicitly and legally excluded from privatization although a number of companies of "strategic importance" require council of ministers' approval before their transformation. Also, the government generally does not plan to dispose of national assets in coal mining, energy supplies and transport infrastructure. Only two pilot projects (Kraków, Opole), both with the participation of foreign capital, exist in the energy sector. During 1994 an intense political discussion continued over the privatization of the tobacco industry, sugar industry and copper mining.

Over recent years several basic techniques for privatising state firms have emerged. The evolution of these variants illustrates the process of adaptation to changing economic, political and social conditions. A specific feature of Polish privatization (as Szomburg also makes clear in his contribution to this volume) is that the initiative and choice of method has largely remained in the hands of the enterprise. The choice of method depends on:

1   the size of the enterprise;
2   projected financial and production indicators;
3   the structure and prospects of the market;
4   interest expressed by Polish and foreign investors.

The privatization law of 13 July 1990 allowed for two fundamental and alternative methods of privatization. One was "commercialization" followed by public sale while the other was "liquidation" and private sale. "Commercialization" involves the transformation of state firms into state treasury corporations (either as joint-stock or limited liability companies) with the shares then sold to private investors. "Privatization through liquidation" takes place according to article 37 of the July 1990 privatization law. This is liquidation with privatization very much in mind unlike the case of liquidation forced by bankruptcy. Usually the subjects are enterprises in relatively good financial condition and for which there are good prospects of finding private interest in purchasing or leasing all or part of the business. The state also makes use of article 19 of the September 1981 law on state firms to try put enterprises which may be in poor financial condition in private hands.

Initial public flotations and trade sales

After transformation of a state-owned enterprise into a joint stock company owned by the treasury comes initial public flotation or trade sales . By law, privatization must occur within a period of no more than two years after commercialization. The minister of privatization may start the privatization process either at the behest of a joint application from the firm's director and workers' council (although the founding body must also approve the plan) or on application of the firm's founding body (so long as the workers' council is consulted and approves). Alternatively the prime minister can initiate privatization if so requested by the privatization minister. Traditional privatization techniques (public flotation, trade sales to Polish or foreign investors, or a combination of the two) are generally applied to large viable enterprises.

Potential buyers of stocks and shares receive a prospectus indicating the value of the business based on a valuation carried out by a specialist firm at the request of the state enterprise. The prospectus also includes the firm's financial statements and future investment plans. It must also fulfil all the requirements of the securities commission regarding the disclosure of economic indicators and financial information expected from publicly traded companies. The 1990 privatization law, still in force at the time of writing in early 1995, allows employees to buy 20 per cent of the total shares at half the public price on the first day of sale, without restricting their right to participate in the general share offer.

Trade sales are managed in the following manner. First, the minister of privatization appoints an adviser (usually one of the advisers working on the sector approach described below). The adviser then prepares the financial and legal audits of the firm, an appropriate information package and seeks potential investors through the mass media and through direct contact with foreign companies. Investors who express an interest receive a detailed memorandum and are asked to present their offer in a bid which should include the proposed price, investment commitments and social plan (employment and wage levels, financing of preferential shares). A list of candidates to be invited to negotiations is then prepared. Prospective purchasers have the right to visit the enterprise for the purpose of their own evaluation.

Privatization through liquidation

A state enterprise can be privatized through liquidation under Article 37 of the July 1990 privatization law by its founding body on the initiative of its workers' council and following approval by the MPW. This allows for three forms of privatization which can be applied separately or jointly. First, the firm can be sold either whole or in part. Second, either all or part of the firm can be transferred into a new joint venture (which may include institutional investors - banks and other financial institutions). This is the form of privatization through liquidation which most frequently involves foreign investors. Third, the firm's assets may be leased, but because of favourable financial conditions, ministry policy restricts this to Polish investors only. A fast track privatization route also exists where an enterprise is sold as a whole but only where the legal ownership of land and other fixed assets under its control has been clearly established. The valuation of the enterprise is simplified by making use, within certain set limits, of an estimate based on its book-value and on annual profits. This accelerates the privatization process and also considerably reduces its cost. But this method is accessible only to Polish investors during the first invitation to negotiations. Should no buyer be found, foreign investors may participate on the same terms as Polish citizens.

Sectoral approach to privatization

The sectoral approach is not a privatization path in itself such as public offering, trade sale, liquidation, buy-out, or a transfer to privatization funds (mass privatization). It can lead to any of those. It can also help initiate co-ordinated actions for company/industry restructuring where appropriate. Therefore, sectoral privatization should be seen mainly as a way of making better informed decision when assigning companies to the various concrete privatization and restructuring paths that are available. Studies on particular industrial sectors have been carried out by the ministry of privatization since mid-1991. These help in the choice of privatization strategy and create a more effective policy towards foreign capital.

The usual approach was to appoint, by competitive tender, a lead adviser, who would perform a domestic and international analysis of the sector and each company in it. At the same time, the adviser contacted potential investors in the sector to gauge their interest and requirements and solicit their ideas about future developments. Finally, the adviser recommended a strategy for the sector and a plan of action for the privatization and/or restructuring of the companies. In this situation firms are sold by the ministry and in this case (unlike privatization through liquidation), the ministry is in the driver's seat and investors benefited from the possibility of one-stop shopping: the adviser negotiates with the investor.

The sectoral approach at its peak in 1992-93 covered 16 branches of Polish industry and some 350 enterprises. Undoubtedly, it provided a better background for decision-making. On the other hand, foreign consultants' dominance in this field was responsible for the "trade sale bias" in policy recommendations. Because of political constraints it could not be the major privatization path in Poland and since 1993, the role of sectoral analysis in privatization has diminished.

Struggle over mass privatization

The mass privatization concept originated in Poland as early as 1988[2]. However, legislation and implementation of the programme were considerably delayed due to political disputes. The mass privatization legislation, the law on national investment funds and their privatization, was finally passed by the Polish parliament in April 1993 and became effective on 14 June 1993.[1] The characteristic feature in Polish mass privatization is the important role played by investment funds in restructuring large scale industry. The restructuring aspect of the PPP[2] is as important as the wide distribution of property rights.

Fifteen National Investment Funds (*Narodowe Fundusze Inwestycjne - NFI*, see Blazyca, p. 15) are to be created, taking the form of closed-end funds registered as joint stock companies. Each *NFI* will be controlled by a supervisory board representing the interests of its shareholders who will all be Polish citizens holding share certificates. The supervisory boards will comprise suitably qualified individuals nominated and appointed by a specially convened selection commission. This selection process took place during the summer of 1994. Two-thirds of the supervisory board's members - including the chairman - will be Polish citizens.

The fund management team behind each *NFI* will report to the supervisory board under a management contract and a performance contract will provide them with financial incentives to increase the long-term value of the fund. Each *NFI* is expected to remain in existence for at least 10 years, partly as a means of ensuring its managers' commitment to the long term.

After the first year, it is intended that each *NFI* will seek a listing on the Warsaw stock exchange. The fund manager will also consider listing the companies in its portfolio if appropriate.

Share holdings in each *NFI* will initially be represented by share certificates, which may be traded immediately in bearer form or converted into "dematerialized" share certificates tradeable on the Warsaw stock exchange. These certificates will also be convertible at a later date for shares in underlying *NFIs*.

In late 1994 the timetable for mass privatization envisaged:

1   the creation of *NFIs* and appointment of fund managers by end 1994;
2   allocation of lead share holdings to *NFIs* by early 1995;
3   distribution of share certificates in 1995;
4   *NFIs* listed on the Warsaw stock exchange and share certificates exchangeable for *NFI* shares in 1996.

In the autumn of 1994, it became clear that there was a serious dispute among the governing coalition partners as to the implementation of the programme. There appeared to be a growing inclination to implement a reduced version of the programme which would be used to compensate both workers in the public sector and pensioners through share certificates. Obviously, such a departure would have nothing in common with the original idea of mass privatization as elaborated by post-Solidarity governments between 1991-93 (see Lewandowski, 1994).

Controversy over restitution of confiscated property

The serious conflicts which delayed mass privatization also suspended the implementation of reprivatization in Poland - that is, compensation for assets confiscated after the Second World War by the communist authorities.

In September 1994 a draft restitution law prepared by the then parliamentary opposition was under consideration in parliament. It consolidated the experiences of the past years. This law anticipated compensation for property confiscated against the law, only for Polish citizens. Under certain conditions the restitution of the actual property, otherwise, some substitute assets or restitution vouchers were to be allocated. However the coalition formed in September 1993 prepared an alternative project which considerably limited restitution since it envisaged only one form of compensation - restitution vouchers. Clearly, no realistic project can cover all cases of confiscation nor satisfy all its victims. Nevertheless, the alternative proposal of the post-communist government seemed to be too limited. It looked certain to provoke the antagonism of the associations of former owners and their families.

Foreign investment in Poland

Foreign parties can invest in Poland in three ways. They can participate in the privatization of the state sector. They can establish a company with 100 per cent foreign participation through greenfield investment. They can co-operate with a Polish private partner.

By the end of June 1994, 17,577 companies with foreign capital participation were registered in Poland. In most cases these were private joint-ventures created by Polish business. Privatized state companies formed the larger partnerships and attracted most of the foreign capital to Poland. The number of companies actually active is of course lower than those registered.

Privatization of course provides an attractive offer for foreign investors - be they active or passive, with large or small capital, starting in business or expanding activities. Foreign investment in privatization can take two basic forms, purchase or joint-venture. With purchase, the capital invested goes to the state treasury - whether through shares or stock of a company sold by capital privatization, or the sale of the whole or part of a firm privatized by liquidation. In the case of a joint-venture on the other hand the capital is invested in the company itself, regardless of the legal status of the Polish partner, whether it be a state owned firm, a state corporation, or an enterprise privatized through liquidation.

Trade sales of entire enterprises and initial public offerings have attracted most of the foreign capital flowing to Poland. Strategic foreign investors have bought stock or shares in more than 50 companies. The largest of these was the sale of 80 per cent of the Kwidzyn paper mill to the US company International Paper for $120 million with further investment commitments of $175 million. The acquisition of the whole or part of a state firm privatized through liquidation is usually a much smaller transaction. One of the largest was the purchase of a machinery repair station near Nowy Targ by a US investor - *Sambud* - for approximately $150,000.

To late 1994, the largest privatization transactions involved the setting up of joint-ventures between a foreign investor and a state treasury corporation. Of approximately 40 such joint-ventures, the most prominent involved Italian capital: Fiat's investment in FSM cars of approximately $180 million with investment commitments of further $1,800 million; and Lucchini's $34.8 million investment and $150m commitments in the Warsaw steel mill.

The setting-up of a joint-venture between a state enterprise and a foreign investor is becoming rare. One of the largest of several hundred such joint-ventures is Coca-Cola Bottlers S.A., set up by Ringnes S.A. from Norway and the state firm Pubrex in Bydgoszcz. Ringnes invested $13.5 million and acquired 80 per cent of the shares in the new venture.

Finally, a joint-venture can be set up between a foreign investor and the state, where the state liquidates the existing enterprise by transferring it into the new company. There have been almost 20 such transactions in Poland the largest involved the construction equipment manufacturer *Metalplast*, in which two Danish investors, Nordisk Wavin (41 per cent) and the Danish Investment Fund for Central and Eastern Europe (10 per cent) invested about $7.6 million.

Altogether, more than $4 billion was invested in Poland by mid-1994. The ranking of our partners is as follows: USA, Italy, Germany, France, Great Britain, Holland. (For more details see: "A Map of the investment risk", 1994). In post-communist Europe, Hungary has attracted most investment while the Czech Republic has a similar experience to Poland.

Privatization results

By the end of 1993, after four years of reforms, Poland's economy was predominantly private, leaving, statistically, the other post-communist countries well behind. By mid-1994 more than 50 per cent of GDP was "privately" produced. Also, 60 per cent of the labour force was employed in the private sector. These figures reflect a dramatic economic and social redistribution of property and deep shifts in the structure of Poland's labour market.

The sectoral penetration of private activity is still highly variable. The private sector accounts for 95 per cent of the labour force in trade and 80 per cent in construction but only 50 per cent in industry and 30 per cent in transport. Remarkably, however, virtually 100 per cent of labour employed outside the rail, air and sea transportation, is in the private sector.

Generally, this dramatic shift in ownership structure in Poland over 1989-93 was mainly produced by "grass-roots" privatization, that is private start-ups. More than 1.5 million out of the 1.8 million existing private businesses were set up over the last four years. But the multi-track programme of privatization has contributed much to these changes, shifting hundreds of state enterprises into private hands.

The number of state owned firms is diminishing systematically, although - parallel to privatization - numerous new public entities are being created generally resulting from the division of existing state-owned conglomerates.

Table 6.1
Number of state firms

Year *	1990	1991	1992	1993	1994
Number	8,441	8,228	7,245	5,924	5,218

Note
*   end year except 1994 when figure is for end June.

At least 2,000 state firms out of the 5,218 registered in mid-1994 were in various stages of a privatization or liquidation procedure. By mid-1994, the impact of privatization was as follows (*Dynamics of Privatization*, 1994):

Table 6.2
Privatization to mid 1994

Method	Number
Capital privatization	115
Privatization through liquidation (mainly employee/management buy-outs)	961
Fast-track privatization (auctions)	100
State firms liquidated due to economic insolvency	1,171

Additionally, more than 1,595 state farms have been deleted from the state enterprise register and transferred to the state treasury agricultural property agency, some 300 transferred into municipal property and at least 400 went bankrupt.

Evaluation of the progress of privatization in Poland

The actual course of privatization appears to be slower and more politically controversial than assumed in 1989-90. Despite this, some 50 per cent of the 8,500 state enterprises existing in 1989, were included in different privatization procedures. In general one can say that the multi-track approach adopted in Poland was successful. It was specifically well tailored to Polish social and economic conditions and the general concept of "bottom-up" privatization.

The strength of organized labour as well as the vital role of managements in state enterprise, well established in the 1980s and discussed more fully by Szomburg in this volume, is reflected in the privatization statistics. It is the insiders - managers and employees - who clearly dominate Polish privatization. Privatization through liquidation, resulting in employee/management buy-outs was initially viewed by the authors of the 1990 privatization law as a marginal privatization route. Trade sales of state firms, transformed into state corporations, was considered to be a far superior privatization method. The outcome however turned these expectations upside down. Liquidation procedures, that is sales involving insiders, were 10 times more numerous than initial public offerings and trade sales. Of course they were also politically less controversial since employees initiated the procedure. On the other hand, the economic impact of this privatization method are dubious and much delayed. Only with time, through the concentration of property rights and with growing financial credibility, will the companies privatized by buy-outs perform better (see Szomburg, Tamowicz, 1993).

From a purely economic standpoint, trade sales involving foreign strategic investors are much more efficient. They entail substantial investments in the form of modernization, restructuring and ecological improvements. They also generate significant budgetary revenues. On the other hand, this privatization path may be more contentious.[3]

The Polish example shows that the privatization is very much a social process - people's perception and the political environment play a significant role. This issue is at the heart of the account given by Szomburg in chapter 5. The greatest victim of the political battles in Poland was no doubt our mass privatization programme, first outlined in 1988-89 and conceptually mature by mid-1991. The implementation of this programme or its further delay will have a decisive impact on the future development of privatization in Poland.

Given the scale of "work in progress" and pressure from enterprises, the post-communist government established in October 1993 is not likely to change substantially the course of privatization in Poland. However, departures from previously clear and transparent procedures, to those favouring domestic bidders can be seen in some sectors of strategic importance as well as in the agro-processing sector.

On the other hand, the dynamic growth of private business, plus the increasing tendency among foreign investors to seek greenfield projects, are becoming more important in the further expansion of the private economy in Poland.

Notes

1   There was however a long struggle over legislative detail which was not resolved until December 1994. It was expected that the scheme would finally be implemented during 1995.

2   *Program Powszechny Prywatyzacja- PPP*. See also Blazyca, chapter 2, p. 15.

3   A more detailed account of Polish privatization processes is provided by the reports regularly prepared by the Gdańsk Institute for Market Economics (see Dąbrowski et al, 1992, 1993).

for Market Economics (see Dąbrowski et al, 1992, 1993).

References

Dąbrowski, J.M., Federowicz, M., Szomburg, J., (1992), "Privatization of Polish State-owned Enterprises", *Economic Transformation*, No. 29, GIME.

Dąbrowski, J.M., Federowicz, M., Kaminiski, T., Szomburg, J., (1993), "Privatization of Polish State-owned Enterprises: Progress, Barriers, Initial Effects", *Economic Transformation*, No. 33, GIME.

Dąbrowski, J.M., (ed), "A Map of Investment Risk", (1994), *Economic Transformation*, No. 43, GIME.

Dynamics of Privatization no. 21, Ministry of privatization, Warsaw, June 1994.

Lewandowski, J., Szomburg, J., (1988), "Privatization as an Foundation of the Socio-economic Reform", in *Proposals of the Transformation of the Polish Economy*, Polish Economic Society, Warsaw.

Lewandowski, J., Szomburg, J., (1990), "The Strategy of Privatization", *Economic Transformation*, No. 7, GIME.

Lewandowski, J., (1994), "The Political Struggle over Mass Privatization in Poland", *Economic Transformation*, No. 46, GIME.

Szomburg, J., Tamowicz, P., (1993), "Proposals for Managers", *Rzeczpospolita*, 5 July 1993.

7 Learning by doing – Entrepreneurs in the first years of the economic transformation

Maciej Grabowski

This chapter offers an overview of small business development in Poland in the period 1990-93, it discusses entrepreneurs' behaviour and their opportunities for future business success. The extent of the private business boom over this period surprised the statistical and fiscal authorities. Small firms have also undoubtedly under-recorded their activities, profit margins, turnover and value-added in order to pay less tax. This means that direct empirical surveys are crucial in tracking the real development of the small and medium-sized enterprise (SME) sector.

Introduction

Ownership changes are the cornerstone of the economic transformation programmes in East European countries. There are three ways of developing private activity in these countries: privatization of existing companies, through foreign direct investment and domestic private business development. These processes are interlinked. If, over 1990-93, privatization of existing companies proceeded more slowly than many hoped, private business development significantly exceeded expectations. Small firms, mainly privately-owned, have flourished and entrepreneurs have easily found a place in the market when legal and economic constraints were eliminated.

The fundamental political changes introduced by the communist authorities after the second world war did not initially affect private SMEs. After the nationalization of larger firms and the appropriation of real estate, the economic situation of SMEs still remained strong. Consumer and investment goods were in great demand in post-war Poland and the population's work ethic was not affected by the communist system. In 1947-48 the private sector produced about 70 per cent of Polish GNP, a figure which declined steadily to less than 20 per cent by 1968.

Centrally planned economies tend to be characterized by having relatively small numbers of enterprises, both small and large. The Czechoslovak case is particularly striking. Historical data on the number of small, medium and large manufacturing enterprises in post-war Czechoslovakia document a trend of ever fewer firms and greater concentration of employment in large enterprises. Even by 1956, 87 per cent of manufacturing employment was located in firms with over 500 workers. By 1988 that proportion rose to 98.6 per cent. During the same period the number of enterprises fell by 43 per cent (see McDermot and Mejstrik, 1992.)

The Polish and Hungarian cases are not as clearly impressive as the Czechoslovak since the number of private small firms was relatively high in these countries. Poland, for instance, had 418,000 private unincorporated businesses in 1985 while Hungary had about 190,000 in 1987. Legal limitations restricted the size of privately owned businesses and so private firms tended to be small and state firms to be large. In Poland, a private firm could not employ more than 50 workers per shift.

Before 1990 small business in Eastern Europe was almost exclusively private and existed on sufferance, only so long as politically tolerated. Two clear trends could be observed: concentration of production in the state sector led to a small number of state firms while private firms' development was restricted. As a result, the number of medium-sized firms was small. Moreover, economic circumstances, especially shortages, influenced private firms' behaviour and they certainly had no need to compete on the world market.

Statistical background

When one takes into consideration that small scale business, especially in trade does not record all sales, and profits are hidden, for instance in personal costs, employment seems to be the best measure of development of this sector (see Table 7.1).

Table 7.1
Private sector employment 1989-91 - Poland, Hungary and Czechoslovakia
(year end, numbers in '000 and % of total employment)

	1989		1990		1991	
	No. (000)	%	No. (000)	%	No. (000)	%
Poland[a]	1,781.4	14.1	4,163.4	33.0	4,503.4	39.0
Hungary[b]	n.a	n.a	1,235	25.3	n.a	n.a
Czechoslovakia	95.0	1.2	499	6.3	1,159	16.4

Notes:
[a] For the non-agricultural sector. The total number of private farmers in 1991 was 3.8 million. Data for 1989 exclude co-operatives, which employed 2.2 million worker in 1989 and 1.5 million in 1990.

[b] Hungarian statistical data do not differentiate between ownership forms but according to the legal form of enterprises. Precise estimates of the private sector are therefore difficult. But assuming that "limited liability" companies are privately owned and that "joint stock" companies are state-owned, it is estimated, that 25.3 per cent of employment was in private sector at the end of 1990.

n.a. - not available.

Sources: Webster, L. (1992a), *Private Sector Manufacturing in Czech and Slovak Federal Republic: A Survey of Firms*, World Bank, December 1992; Webster, L (1992c), *Private Sector Manufacturing in Poland: A survey of Firms*, World Bank, December 1992; Zoltan, R. (1992), 'Hungary', in Piasecki, B. (ed.), *Politics of SMEs development in Central and Eastern Europe*, 19th International Small Business Congress, Warsaw 1992; *Rocznik Statystyczny* 1992, (GUS Warszawa 1992) pp.XIII, XIV and own calculations.

The data show that the share of private sector employment expanded rapidly in these speedily reforming countries to reach between 16 per cent and 39 per cent of total employment in 1991. The fastest growth was in the former Czechoslovakia, where small business was weakly developed prior to 1990. Of course it should be noted that these data are related to the currently employed labour force. Unemployment rose sharply in the countries concerned in recent years, from virtually zero in 1989 to 11.8 per cent in Poland in 1991, to 7.5 per cent in Hungary and 6.6 per cent in Czechoslovakia as the state sector began to shrink.

After 1989 all three countries adopted similar legal forms based on their pre-war commercial codes for businesses. These were based on the German and Austrian business tradition. The legal form of business is similar in all three countries: joint stock companies, limited liability companies and unincorporated firms may all exist. The data in Table 7.2 show changes in the numbers of incorporated and unincorporated firms over the 1989-92 period.

From an economic viewpoint incorporated firms are presumably more important because of their greater average size and better development potential. For instance, in 1989 the average private incorporated firm in Poland had 19.5 employees with only 1.8 employees in unincorporated firms. Capital requirements are also higher for incorporated companies than for unincorporated ones. At the end of 1992 the minimum capital requirement for a limited liability company was, in Czechoslovakia, Kcs100,000 or approximately $3,900 in Hungary it was Forints 1,000,000 or $12,000 in Hungary, and in Poland 40 million złoty or around $2,660. The ratio of the number of incorporated private firms per 1,000 citizens is useful in comparing the potential of the private sector. In 1992, this ratio was 1.4 for Poland, 4.2 for Czechoslovakia and 5.6 for Hungary.

The Polish private sector is dominated by unincorporated firms with a small number of incorporated companies. Czechoslovakia and Hungary have better balances in this respect. Some explanation of that difference is the tax exemption granted to newly established unincorporated firms introduced in May 1990 in Poland. It is interesting too that the minimum capital needed to establish a limited liability company lowest in Poland. The Hungarian requirement is nearly five times greater. Surveys show the average replacement value of equipment in industrial private firms was $320,500 in Hungary, $244,537 in Czechoslovakia and $132,321 in Poland (Webster, 1992a). By and large, Hungarian and Czechoslovak firms are better capitalized than small private Polish concerns.

Table 7.2
Private sector growth in Poland, Hungary and
Czechoslovakia 1989-92
Number of private firms

	1989	1990	1991	1992
		[a] Incorporated Firms		
Poland	11.7	29.6	45.1	51.2
Hungary[c]	4.5	18.3	41.2	57.3
Czechoslovakia[d]	0.2	12.2	39.0	43.5
		[b] Unincorporated Firms		
Poland	813	1,135	1,420	1,523
Hungary[c]	186.3	234.0	300.0	na
Czechoslovakia[d]	86.8	468.4	1,175	1,262

Notes:

[a] Incorporated firms cover limited liability companies and joint stock companies, including privatized companies.

[b] Unincorporated firms cover is sole proprietors and partnerships.

[c] Presumably most limited liability companies are privately-owned and most joint stock companies are state-owned. In Hungary there are about 35 times more limited liability companies than joint stock companies.

[d] Includes state-owned incorporated firms. According to L.Webster (1992a p.13) about 2/3 of all incorporated firms is privately owned in Czechoslovakia, so the probable number of private incorporated firms is 33,000 at September, 1992.

Sources: Webster, L., op. cit, Table 1; Grabowski, M., Kulawczuk, P. (1992), "Small and Medium-sized Enterprises in Poland - Analysis and Policy Recommendations", *The Gdańsk Institute for Market Economics*; *Statisztikai havi Kozlemenyek*, December 1992, Budapest 1993; *Biuletyn statystyczny*, 11/1992, GUS Warszawa 1992; *Short-term economic statistics Central and Eastern Europe*, OECD, Paris 1992.

Evidence also points to a different external environment facing private business in the countries under discussion. Empirical surveys show that Polish private firms compete and trade mostly among themselves while in Hungary and Czechoslovakia they rely on state enterprises as main customers and suppliers. In Czechoslovakia the state sector is the main competitor for private firms; in Hungary private business competes with both the state and private sectors while in Poland the private sector competes against and within itself and the informal sector.

It should also be noted that the very high number of unincorporated firms in Poland and Czechoslovakia does not necessarily mean that they are all actually operating or providing a main source of income for their owners. This suggests that the average size of unincorporated firms is presumably more than merely 2 employees. Some firms may be "shells" registered only for future use or temporarily utilised by self-employed owners[1]. For all three countries the rapid growth in the number of private businesses in the early stage of transformation confirms firstly that many people have been eager to become entrepreneurs and secondly that it has been fairly easy to find a place on the market.

The entrepreneur and business expectations

We noted earlier that statistical data on SMEs are not reliable in the transformation period. This means that direct empirical surveys are of great importance. The Gdańsk Institute carried out three cross-country surveys in June and December 1991 and in June 1992 to obtain an immediate view and information on Polish *private sector* SMEs. These surveys covered 207, 299 and 272 enterprises across a wide range of sectors and were carried out in Kraków, Łódz and Gdańsk-Gdynia (the first was carried out only in Łódz and Gdańsk-Gdynia). The data from the December 1991 survey are referred to here since that questionnaire was the most comprehensive and the sample the most numerous.

The sample was selected at random, independently across three groups by firm size: 5-10 employees, 10-20 and 20-100. Because there were more small companies (5-10 employees) than big ones (over 20 employees), the choice of firms was skewed in favour of larger companies. The idea was to examine a cross-section of various types of SMEs. As the surveys got underway we had to select additional firms for a variety of reasons: on occassion the statistical office had the wrong address (56 per cent of such cases), sometimes enterprises refused to participate in surveys (15 per cent), and sometimes individuals competent to complete the questionnaire were simply absent (28 per cent). On average 180 firms were selected in order to complete 100 questionnaires. The rule was to try to keep the same firms in three consecutive surveys but this was not always possible (about 30 per cent of firms were replaced). All sectors were represented in the surveys. In the December 1991 sample 30 per cent were engaged in trade, 27 per cent in manufacturing, 26 per cent in services, 12 per cent in construction and 5 per cent were multi-branch firms.

What did our surveys show? First, Polish entrepreneurs are well-educated (two-thirds of them had a university degree). Second, they are middle aged. There are more business people over 50 years old than there are under 30 years. Third, many are experienced. Over 40 per cent had occupied managerial posts in state-owned enterprises before they opened their own business. This certainly helped them take the first steps in independent business since they would have easy access to skilled people, business contacts and sometimes access to good contracts previously taken by state companies. The former managers of state firms, today's entrepreneurs, tried to use their own newly established firms to replace some of the transactions previously concluded between state firms and their commercial partners. Fourth, very few Polish business people (only 2.5 per cent) returned from abroad to run businesses in Poland. Fifth, women are very under represented and make up only around 10 per cent of all private sector small business.

As might be expected Polish SMEs are young; most of them are less than 5 years old. Our random sample contained only 10 per cent firms established before 1980. Entrepreneurs are highly and positively motivated persons. They started their businesses to increase their incomes, to fulfil personal ambitions and to be independent. Our surveys rarely showed negative stimuli, for instance anxieties over redundancy or unemployment, to be important. Entrepreneurs relied mainly on their own savings to establish businesses. Informal loans from relatives or friends and foreign currency savings were other common source of initial capital.

Polish entrepreneurs have gained the necessary skills to run businesses in a learning-by-doing process. The experience of working in state-owned concerns functioning in the shortage economy cannot be directly and usefully transferred to small private firms in the transformed economy of the 1990s.

Businessmen are rather optimistic as to their future and their development opportunities. Over half of those in our sample wanted to invest, two fifths wanted to build new facilities and nearly half wanted to buy new machines or technology. This displays a conviction and confidence in an ability to run bigger businesses. Even more of our respondents believed it essential to increase their firms' size, in the form of turnover or fixed capital. Most predicted there would be an increase in competition and concentration in their area of business and they felt they had to expand their business in order to survive. However, entrepreneurs were not content with all the changes taking place in the competitive environment. Their views on privatization, based on our June 1992 survey across 272 firms, may be of particular interest.

Private business clearly had strong views on the privatization programme: a minority of business people declared indifference on this issue. With regard to conditions on the labour and consumer markets the majority response indicated that privatization was unwelcome. This is probably because of the unwelcome impact of increased competition, of course, a desirable phenomenon from a broader economic perspective. Privatization brings with it increased competition in the labour market (for skilled employees) and in consumer markets and this no businessman likes. On the other hand businessmen are happy to see greater competition on the supplier side of the market.

Privatization is to a certain extent synonymous with the economic transformation process. Yet private sector development in Poland follows two tracks which rarely cross. The privatization programme is not addressed to private entrepreneurs and their participation in it is very limited. Table 7.4 shows the current and anticipated participation of SMEs in privatization.

Some 38 per cent of firms sampled (103 from 272) were already actively involved in the privatization process in some way. Over half (148) anticipated some future participation in the programme. Thus, while privatization attracts the attention of many entrepreneurs their actual involvement tends to be smaller. The survey also highlights two striking features. First, a considerable number of businesses anticipated that they might acquire an enterprise. Second, although leasing state assets was relatively important in the past it appears to be considered much more rarely for the future. Finally, becoming involved in privatization through share purchases in public flotations has always been the least attractive option although more respondents have expressed a willingness to buy shares in the future than in the past.

Table 7.3
Entrepreneurs' views on the privatization programme

Question:
In which way, in your opinion, have privatization programmes carried out
in Poland affected the following: the labour market, the supplier market,
the consumer market?

The impact of privatization on:	favourable	unfavourable	indifferent
labour market	35%	39%	25%
consumer market	27%	55%	18%
supplier market	61%	19%	19%

Note: Figures may not add to 100 because of rounding.
Source: Own calculation based on a survey of 272 firms carried out in
June 1992.

Table 7.4
**Current and anticipated participation of SMEs
in the privatization programme**

Question:
Have you participated in the privatization programme?
if so, in what way:

(i)   acquired or merged with a state firm
(ii)   purchase of shares in a state firm
(iii)   leased facilities or machinery from a state firm
(iv)   purchase fixed assets from liquidated state firms

Question:
Are you planning to:

(i)   acquire or merge with a state firm
(ii)   purchase of shares in a state firm
(iii)   lease facilities or machinery from a state firm
(iv)   purchase fixed assets from liquidated state firms

Participation in privatization by:	At present	Plans
acquiring or merging with state enterprise	4%	21%
purchase of shares in public flotations	1%	6%
lease of facilities or machinery	25%	13%
purchase of fixed assets from a liquidated state firm	14%	27%

Note: more then one answer was allowed.
Source: Own calculation based on a survey of 272 firms carried out in
June 1992.

SMEs, their rivals and their customers

The small firm's market position and share depends very much on the intensity of the competition it faces. Polish SMEs compete mainly against other small firms and illegal traders. They operate in a market which consists of private firms and so private businesses are locked in competition with other private enterprises while state-owned companies compete with other state firms. Our surveys (see Table 7.5) show that in the view of the SMEs themselves their major source of rivalry is clearly other private firms: these provided 36 per cent of the competition in 1992. Next comes the illegal sector of unregistered firms with almost 22 per cent of the competition. State owned companies provided 13.8 per cent, and importers 9.8 per cent of the competition respectively. Surveys of SMEs in 1991 and 1992 also show that the role of state-owned firms as customers of small private business is diminishing. Concentration of sales was high but it has also become clear that fewer SMEs depend on one big customer. In the 1992 survey, 42 per cent of firms declared that a main customer was responsible for more than 30 per cent of total sales while in 1991 the proportion of firms reporting the same level of sales concentration was 46 per cent.

The state sector is much more important as a supplier to SMEs than it is as a consumer. This, of course, results from the dominant position of the state in certain sectors, for example, its monopoly position in the energy market. Nevertheless, the most important suppliers for SMEs are private firms with state enterprise running a close second. Co-operation links between small private business and the state sector are relatively weak and this is due to the poor financial condition of state firms.

Private SMEs tend to operate on local markets. Our survey indicated that in 1991 65.3 per cent of all sales were confined to the county in which the firm operated. Just under 30 per cent of sales were on the national market and, not surprisingly, only the manufacturing companies in our sample sell more on the national market then on the local one. As might be expected the value of goods exported by SMEs is not high (around 5 per cent of total sales). These data are recorded below in Table 7.6.

Table 7.5
Private sector perceptions of competition*

Main rivals	% June 1992	% Dec 1991
other private companies	36.3	34.0
unregistered firms (that is illegal traders)	21.7	19.3
state-owned companies	13.8	15.6
importers	9.8	12.3
no rivals	7.4	6.9
co-operatives	3.1	4.8
foreign companies	5.2	4.5
others	2.6	2.7
total	100.0	100.0

Note: * Respondents were asked to define no more than three significant types of competitor for their company starting from the most significant (that is the main competitor scored "1", the second one "2", and the third one "3"). Competitors were subsequently ranked - according to importance - from which a total was established, and the effectiveness of competition from various sectors was calculated.
Source: Own calculations based on surveys in December 1991 and June 1992.

Table 7.6
Geographical pattern of sales by private sector small businesses in 1991

Radius of market	% of sales
Local market (county)	65.3
National market	29.7
Former COMECON countries	1.1
Western countries	4.1

Source: Own calculations based on survey in December 1991

Marketing skills seem to be poorly developed in the SME sector. Our surveys showed that SMEs were more familiar with their suppliers than their customers. Yet for the future marketing skills are likely to be critical since competition will intensify. Where entrepreneurs have made efforts to improve their position on the market these have largely been based on intuition. Most of them spend very little on promotion and advertising although in 1991 and 1992 such expenditure did increase in real terms and also grew faster than sales. The SME sector is convinced of the necessity of marketing activity but where it exists it is not carried out in a planned or systematic manner.

Financing SMEs

Statistical data on the financial situation of SMEs may be particularly misleading and the source of much confusion. The division of personal and firm assets is often not clear. SMEs are also able to conceal their profits and turnover. And they do so for many reasons. Our surveys however give some insight into SME financing. First, small firm have expanded at a fast pace. The firms in our sample pointed to a 16-fold increase in the value of capital employed[2]. A much faster expansion occurred among service sector companies where firms reported an increase in assets of 25 times their initial value although it should be noted that the starting point for this expansion was low; service sector firms have a notoriously low assets base. Trading firms expanded at a relatively slow pace: an 11-fold increase in assets.

The SME sector relies heavily on a steady cash flow from sales and indeed most sales are carried out for cash - 55 per cent of all sales for our sampled firms. This is a result of problems with maintaining financial liquidity. Some 48 per cent of companies declared they held debts over a month old amounting to 45 per cent of all debts. Of course, state companies and agencies are more intensive holders of overdue debt than private companies. This creates a situation where private companies are more creditworthy despite the fact that they are small entities. An example of the sort of situation common for small firms is given by one Gdańsk based concern owed money by the Polish Army for goods delivered six months earlier. Eventually the company received an offer from the army for speedy settlement but on condition of annulment of the contractual penalties for delay.

All businessmen complain about taxes but the average profits tax paid by SMEs is low, despite the fact that its formal rate is 40 per cent. This is due to the great scope that exists to reduce reported profits by overestimating overheads. Taxes on wages and national insurance contributions exceed the combined total of sales and profit taxes. In terms of tax burden private companies paid little in local and direct taxes, a moderate amount in indirect and wage taxes but faced high levels of national insurance contributions. Not surprisingly, business people considered the fairest taxes to be those that are the lowest, that is, the local and direct taxes, with national insurance, in their opinion, the most unfair tax.

But one must recall that the tax system has loopholes which can be exploited legally or illegally. One manner of tax evasion deserves fuller description. Trading companies established in 1990 enjoyed total relief from tax payments for 3 years. The exemption could be used by non-trading companies too if they co-operated or sold to these tax-exempt trade companies. Take by way of example a manufacturing firm selling to a trading firm. They may agree on a real market price for the product delivered by the manufacturing concern but the price on the invoice is, say, was 30 per cent lower. Frequently the manufacturing firm does not have any profits on its books while in reality the trade firm pays the missing part of the agreed price "under the table" to the manufacturer. The parallel is obvious with the transfer pricing technique used by multinationals to reduce their total tax liabilities.

SMEs are not major clients of the banks. The difficulty in accessing credit and lengthy transaction times are criticisms commonly made by small businesses. Our research showed that one out of five companies used bank credit facilities, two thirds of which for working capital. Only 8 per cent of the 299 companies sampled in December 1991 used more than one type of credit facility. An analysis of loans offered showed significant diversity both in their value and in the level of interest rates. In 1990-91 the interest rates on working capital ranged from 36 per cent to 108 per cent (omitting hard currency credits at 14 per cent). The weighted average rate was 55.5 per cent.

Credit facilities were not common tools for financing business and 70 per cent of companies did not even attempt to obtain credit. Undoubtedly, this was due to the high level and spread of interest rates. Access to subsidised credit strengthens informal but corrupt relationships between bank officers and entrepreneurs. Besides high interest rates entrepreneurs complained that banks required excessive collateral with some forms of collateral not accepted at all. Interviews with banking officers confirmed this. Banks are reluctant to accept some collateral because of weaknesses of the legal system (for instance residential and eviction laws are not robust enough to permit housing to be used as security for bank loans).

Conclusions

The early stage of the transformation process was associated with a remarkable development of private sector business. But this has now passed as easy-to-fill market niches have vanished. The period of quick and easy profits associated with the decline of the centrally planned economy and with hyperinflation are finished and will not return. The Polish private sector consists of small and very small firms; the number of medium-sized firm is low. This is a rather unexpected outcome of economic policy towards small business, including tax exemptions granted to small unincorporated trading businesses.

The average profit rate in private firms established three or four years ago was high and the smallest of small firms expanded far more rapidly (in terms of assets) than did the SME sector as a whole. After a period when trading enterprises developed most rapidly the outlook for industrial and service companies gradually improved. Simultaneously, big firms started to do better in relation to small firms in terms of profitability. By and large entrepreneurial pioneers were well rewarded for taking the risk of starting a business in the beginning of the transformation period.

Private firms are eager to participate in privatization programmes in an active manner. Over half of the entrepreneurs interviewed expressed a desire to take part in privatization. For small business leasing was the easiest way into privatization but in the future this is likely to be replaced by the outright purchase of the assets of liquidated enterprises. Companies seldom use credit to finance their current activity and even less so to finance investment. The process of getting loans is not considered to be unduly long but is tiresome and poorly managed. For private firms the cost of credit is well above the bank's base rate. Collateral can be difficult to find. Bills of exchange are generally not accepted by the banks.

Lack of financial liquidity is one of the most dramatic problems facing small firm. It also reflects the low financial skill of managers. Over half of businesses sampled reported receivables to be overdue and the most common debtors are state firms. This phenomenon combined with the high cost of working capital has encouraged SMEs to carry out transactions for cash.

The greatest tax burden stems from social security contributions rather than sales or profits tax. This pattern of the incidence of taxation points to private firms as being labour-intensive with low declared profitability. Businesses complained that social security and local taxes were the most harmful (there are numerous ways to evade profits and sales taxes though a tendency to declare lower turnover and higher costs than really exists). Firms pay little in profits taxation but this evasion (lower declared profits) hampers them when they look for bank loans.

Small and medium-sized private enterprises were, and are, entities where thousands of people learned how the market worked. This enrichment of human capital is perhaps one of the most important aspects of the transition which was launched in Poland in 1990. It is also worth noting that today the capital and skill requirements needed to start a business are much harder to ignore or avoid than in the earliest phase of transformation.

Notes

1   Johnson argues that the high number of self-employed individuals in Czechoslovakia was boosted by exempting them from 50 per cent wages tax. This led large private firms to encourage their workers to become self-employed, Johnson, S. (1992): *Private Business in Eastern Europe*, World Bank, Research Paper Series, p.9.

2   The initial capital and the present value of the firm were estimated by businessmen in current prices then deflated by the consumer prices index.

3   In 1991 and 1992 the tax regime for SMEs consisted of three parts. A lump sum tax applied to very small family firms with fewer than 4 employees. A simple taxation method was applied to businesses with limited annual turnover (6 billion złoty). Corporation income tax was levied on the profits of incorporated companies or businesses with turnover greater than 6 billion złoty. In 1994 the tax system includes a lump sum tax (as above), businesses with lower annual turnover than 1.2 billion złoty pay tax on sales, (trade firms pay 2.5 per cent on their declared sales, manufacturing and construction pay 5 per cent on sales and services pay 7.5 per cent on sales). This does not provide any incentive to reveal total turnover for these small businesses. Incorporated companies pay 40 per cent corporation tax.

References

Johnson, S. (1992): *Private Business in Eastern Europe*, World Bank, Research Paper Series, p.9.

McDermott, G., M.Mejstrik (1992), "The Role of Small Firms in the Industrial Development and Transformation of Czechoslovakia", **Small Business Economics**, 4/1992, pp. 179-199.

8 The role of the financial system in supporting economic development

Zbigniew Polański

Introduction

In the past the financial system was one of the basic features distinguishing the capitalist market economy from the socialist economy. Indeed, socialism aimed at eliminating money and financial relations from its economic system. In 1919 Bukharin and Preobrazhensky (1974, p.37) declared for example that "Communist society will know nothing of money". In practice however despite attempts to eliminate money (as in Soviet Russia in 1918-21 or in Cambodia in the 1970s) socialist economies used money and had financial systems. Nevertheless, the role performed by money was definitely different and the financial system did not resemble that of developed market economies.

In Poland the late 1980s saw rapid development of a market-type financial system, based on really functioning financial markets and profit-oriented financial institutions. This is a natural process since money and the financial system perform an important role in market economies. But did the financial system, even in the first half of the 1990s, already have a positive impact on development of the Polish economy?

The present study outlines some of the problems that emerged in the development of the Polish financial system after 1990, that is, since the moment when a conscious decision was made to embark on a consistent systemic transformation aimed at creating a capitalist system in Poland. Following this introduction part two below provides a description of this process, concentrating primarily on the development of organizational and legal structures in the new financial system. We also highlight some quantitative features of financial system development. In section three we offer a more qualitative review. Section four is an attempt to evaluate the evolution of the financial system from the point of view of its impact on wider economic development, its impact on inflation and recession in 1990 and 1991 as well as on the gradual recovery that emerged from 1992. The study ends with a summary offering also some remarks on most recent developments.

Development of the Polish financial system: organizational and legal considerations

The starting point

In Poland the movement from the command economy started in earnest in the early 1980s as a result of the challenges posed by Solidarity in 1980 and 1981. Despite the imposition in December 1991 of martial law (and the banning of Solidarity) attempts to reform the socialist economic system were undertaken a year later. Consequently, Poland's extremely centralized financial system typical of command economies began slowly to disintegrate from 1982 (see Polański, 1991, 1995). This does not mean, however, that the early 1980s saw the emergence of a new market-type financial system; that process began only in 1988-89.

The last two communist governments in office accelerated institutional change and, as a result, Polish reforms became increasingly market based. This was true too of the financial system. Banking reform was a key element in this process. At the end of January 1989 Parliament passed two key pieces of banking legislation: a new general banking Act and the Central Bank (National Bank of Poland - NBP) Act.

As a consequence of the latter the National Bank divested itself of its regional branch structure and began to concentrate on central banking functions as conventionally understood. This led, on February 1, 1989 to the nine branches of the NBP starting operations as independent entities thus marking the departure from the "mono-bank" system typical of socialist economies and the transition to a two-tier (central bank - commercial banks) system typical of market economies.

Meanwhile the Polish Banking Act was modelled on German legislation and this law, like similar laws passed in other post-communist countries (for further details see Blommenstein and Spencer, 1994, pp. 163-8), creates the basis for universal banking, financial institutions not only accepting deposits and creating credit, but also offering a wide range of other financial services although mainly in investment banking.

The 1989 Banking Act permitted the establishment of new banks organized as joint-stock companies with the participation of both Polish and foreign parties. In early 1989 the NBP started to issue licenses for new banks. These were mainly established by state-owned enterprises and local government. For more on changes in the banking system in Poland over 1986-94 see Table 8.1.

These banking reforms took place at a most difficult time. In late 1989 a hyperinflation emerged and over 1990-91 the economy was to take a nose-dive towards an unprecedented economic crash.

The financial system after 1990

The economic policy of the first non-communist government initially focused on macroeconomic stabilization. A restrictive macroeconomic policy was accompanied by a sweeping liberalization of economic activity. Most state-controlled prices were freed and the złoty became convertible for all current account transactions. Despite the limitations of this purely "internal convertibility" this did mean the end of the state's monopoly of foreign trade and from the beginning of 1990 the Polish economy has been internationally open.

With priorities focused on macroeconomic problems and liberalization relatively little attention was devoted to the financial system. Policy here concentrated on liberalising the rules regulating the establishment of new financial institutions and on removing administrative obstacles to existing institutions' operation. For example, in 1990 an Act was passed permitting the (more than 1,600, see Table 8.1) co-operative banks that used to be strictly supervised by the state-co-operative Bank Gospodarki Żywnościowej (the Agricultural Bank) to leave the BGŻ structure. In the summer of 1990 a new law on insurance companies created conditions for the quick development in numbers of companies in this sector. At the end of 1990 the privatization of state-owned enterprises was started. April 1991 saw the launch of the Warsaw stock exchange. At the same time the NBP conducted a very liberal bank licensing policy leading, in 1990 alone, to 45 licenses for the establishment of new banks.

Table 8.1
Banks active in Poland, 1986-94 (selected years)

Item	1986	1989	1990	1991	1992	1993	1994[d]
Total[a]	4	21	53/1716	76/1743	87/1752	90/1754	86/1716
State-owned banks	4	17	16	16	15	13	13
Central bank	1	1	1	1	1	1	1
State banks	-	11	11	2	2	2	2
Joint-stock companies	2	4	3	12	11	9	9
State-co-operative bank[b]	1	1	1	1	1	1	1
Private sector banks[c] of which:	-	4	37	60	71	74	70
Foreign banks	-	-	3	6	6	7	7
Branches of foreign banks	-	-	-	-	2	3	3
Co-operative banks	662	662	1663	1667	1665	1664	1630
Integrated into the BGŻ structure	662	662	1578	1575	1481	1270	1212
Outside the BGŻ structure	-	-	85	92	184	394	418
Privatized banks	-	-	-	-	1	3	3

Note: The data in the Table refers to active entities, i.e. banks which were really conducting banking operations and reporting to NBP. Thus their increases from 1989 are not equal to the number of licenses issued each year by NBP.

a   Since 1990 the second figure includes all co-operative banks.

b   Bank Gospodarki Żywnościowej (BGŻ) (Agricultural Bank). In 1993 54 per cent of its capital was held by the State and the remaining 46 per cent by the co-operative banks. In the fall of 1994 it was incorporated as a joint stock-company with 66 per cent of capital belonging to the State and the rest to co-operative banks.

c   Created on the basis of the 1989 Banking Act.

d   As of August.

Source: National Bank of Poland

Table 8.2

Structure of credits granted to the non-financial sector by Polish commercial banks 1989-1994 (in %)

Item	1989	1990	1991	1992	1993	1994[f]
All Banks	100.0	100.0	100.0	100.0	100.0	100.0
State-owned[a]	95.9	89.4	81.4	77.8	68.3	67.5
Four largest banks[b]	50.1	44.4	42.3	43.1	43.3	42.3
Banks separated from NBP in 1989[c]	45.5	43.3	37.3	34.6	25.0	25.1
Other	0.3	1.6	1.9	0.1	0.1	0.1
Private sector banks[c]	0.2	3.2	9.1	12.5	16.3	17.1
Co-operative	3.9	7.4	9.5	8.4	7.0	7.2
Privatized[e]	-	-	-	1.3	8.3	8.2

Note: Figures may not add to 100.0 due to rounding error.
[a] Including Bank Gospodarki Żywnościowej (Agricultural Bank), a state-co-operative partnership.
[b] Bank Handlowy w Warszawie S.A., Bank Polska Kasa Opieki S.A., Powszechna Kasa Oszczędności-BP (State Savings Bank) and Bank Gospodarki Żywnościowej (Agricultural Bank).
[c] Nine banks until 1992. In the 1993 and 1994 figures the two privatized banks are excluded.
[d] Banks created on the basis of the 1989 Banking Act.
[e] In 1992 - Bank Rozwoju Eksportu S.A., in 1993 - Wielkopolski Bank Kredytowy S.A. and Bank Śląski S.A.
[f] As of August.

Source: National Bank of Poland.

As a result of these developments, a three-tier banking system emerged consisting of: state-owned banks; new, largely private banks established on the basis of the 1989 Banking Act; and the co-operative banks emerging from the strict hold of the Agricultural Bank, BGŻ (see Kloc, 1993, pp 7-17). By 1994 this three-tier structure characterised the Polish banking system although privatization also started to have an impact.

General economic liberalization in 1990 did not have a great impact on bank-enterprise relations. The banks however faced problems. They were poorly endowed with capital and their decision-making was often careless. In 1991 a new stage of financial system reform switched the emphasis from establishment of new banks to the re-organization and privatization of institutions owned by the state treasury. In late 1991 the nine banks that had (in 1989) been carved out of the old NBP were reconstituted as joint-stock companies with subsequent privatization very much in mind. In the summer of 1992 the first bank privatization took place. This was not one of the original "NBP nine" mentioned earlier. It was only in 1993 that two of these banks were privatized. Meanwhile the number of licenses for the establishment of new banks fell from 18 in 1991, to 6 in 1992 and to only one each in 1993 and 1994.

As regards non-deposit financial institutions, reform in the insurance sector followed the pattern in banking. Here, as with banking, after widespread liberalization, attention shifted to institutional and legal changes and to some extent also to privatization. The largest Polish insurance company, (the equivalent in insurance of the socialist mono-bank) was incorporated as a joint-stock company with its life insurance branch hived off. In 1993, the second-largest insurance company, was privatized. The first and only trust fund in Poland began operating in 1992.

These changes in the financial system were accompanied by some negative features. Like other countries undergoing sweeping financial liberalization without appropriate legal safeguards and effective supervision (see Díaz-Alejandro, 1985), Poland soon faced some serious problems. In March 1992, one new private bank, was closed and in 1993 the third-largest insurance company in the country, was closed. Co-operative banks were the hardest-hit by the crisis (see Table 8.1). In mid-1994 21 banks (co-operative banks excluded) had a capital adequacy ratio below 8 per cent, that is, below the Basle Committee on Banking Supervision norm.

The year 1994 witnessed the transition to the next stage of financial system development in Poland. This was shaped by a number of factors including the poor capital endowment of Polish financial institutions as well as an awareness that Poland's Association Agreement with the EC in March 1992 required an opening of the Polish financial market to foreign competition in 1997. The collapse of some banks together with fears of future competition have pushed the Polish financial sector towards greater consolidation. The first merger occurred in 1992 after the bankruptcy of one minor bank. However it was only in 1994 that financial institutions began systematically to develop better co-operation. Reform in the co-operative banking sector should also be viewed in this context. The structure of this sector of Polish banking is the subject of intensive changes. In September 1994 a decision was made on incorporating the BGŻ bank as a joint-stock company. The BGŻ is to be deeply, with technical assistance from the World Bank, financially and organizationally restructured. Co-operative banks are to be consolidated and their area of operation restricted.

Tables 8.1 and 8.2 provide an insight to the banking system's evolution in recent years. However, the rapid growth in bank numbers was accompanied by only slow changes in the structure of credits granted to the non-financial sector (see Table 8.2). Most of these credits still come from state-owned banks. Similarly in the insurance sector in 1993 more than 75 per cent of all premiums were collected by the two largest state-owned firms. It is also worth noting that these changes had no effect whatsoever on the social insurance system. Its operation in 1994 was still based on socialist economy principles. It still relied on obligatory premiums paid only by employers. As the premiums are among the highest in Europe (their rate in 1994 was equivalent to 48 per cent of the average wage) they constitute a heavy burden for companies. At the same time, however, the social insurance system is in permanent deficit which is covered by state budget subsidies.

From 1990 the market for long-term securities, both shares and treasury bonds also developed. By the end of 1994, more than 30 company stocks as well as a variety of treasury bonds were listed on the Warsaw stock exchange. But it is worth noting that the market in corporate bonds has not developed at all and neither has the market for short-term enterprise debt. Treasury bills and interbank deposits were the only money market instruments. It is a characteristic feature of the Polish money market that its interbank segment has developed relatively smoothly, while transactions in other short-term instruments are insignificant. Thus Polish financial markets remain in a fledgling state and this is reflected, among others, in its uneven development and its substantial segmentation (Polański, 1994b).

From the moment of departure from the mono-bank system in 1989 the number of financial institutions and instruments grew markedly.

Nevertheless, in a number of fields (social insurance, some segments of financial markets, for example the non-bank money market) there have been little or no changes. Moreover the symptoms of a deep crisis in financial institutions have been evident since 1991.

Development of the Polish financial system: qualitative considerations

Let us now approach the evolution of the Polish financial system from the point of view of such a system in a market economy. In the West financial functions may be grouped into three major categories: monetary, control and capital. Financial systems in market economy always perform these functions, although they may be carried out by means of a wide range of institutional solutions (Rybczynski, 1992 pp. 254-5).

Monetary functions

The new economic policy launched in January 1990 totally changed the policy hitherto pursued by Poland's central bank. The NBP was no longer simply a passive supplier of money for the economy since control over macroeconomic financial aggregates (money and credit supply) aimed at checking inflation became the essence of its activity. However, the effectiveness of this new macroeconomic policy was itself subject to changes in the nature of the financial system. It is only in a system with well-functioning banks and financial markets that the central bank can hope to influence the microeconomic level since financial markets and institutions transmit central bank incentives to economic agents.

The financial system in the socialist economy performed purely monetary tasks; it managed the money supply and facilitated settlements between non-financial agents. But all of this was done passively since in the centrally planned economy financial flows were subordinate to tangible (real) flows. Moreover, the supply of credit and money flows were controlled by administrative measures such as simple rationing. This of course led to problems in managing a new economic policy.

From 1990 monetary policy aimed to restrict money and credit supply growth. At first it was assumed that these objectives would be achieved by using the interest rate (on refinancing credits) and reserve requirements ratios as major instruments. Later, open market operations would assume greater importance. Tables 8.3 and 8.4 show that despite a very high level of nominal interest rates, especially in the early 1990s, the central bank's policy was in fact only moderately restrictive. In particular, real interest rates in 1990 were still clearly negative, while the supply of money and credit was rising very rapidly. It is clear from table 8.4 that money and credit supply growth rates for the non-financial sector were divergent throughout the whole 1990-94 period. This was because in some years money supply growth was heavily influenced by the state budget deficit and foreign settlements. For further details see Polański (1993 and 1994a).

Table 8.3

Inflation and the National Bank of Poland basic interest rate 1989-94

Item	1989	1990	1991	1992	1993	1994
All Banks	100.0	100.0	100.0	100.0	100.0	100.0
State-owned[a]	95.9	89.4	81.4	77.8	68.3	67.5
Four largest banks[b]	50.1	44.4	42.3	43.1	43.3	42.3
Banks separated from NBP in 1989[c]	45.5	43.3	37.3	34.6	25.0	25.1
Other	0.3	1.6	1.9	0.1	0.1	0.1
Private sector banks[c]	0.2	3.2	9.1	12.5	16.3	17.1
Co-operative	3.9	7.4	9.5	8.4	7.0	7.2
Privatized[e]	-	-	-	1.3	8.3	8.2

Note: NBP basic interest rate is understood here as average yearly interest rate on NBP's refinancing credits.
[a] Cumulative monthly indexes.
[b] Forecast.
[c] Yearly average based on January-August 1994 period rate.
[d] The deflator is based on price indexes covering January-August 1994 period.
Source: National Bank of Poland and Polish Central Statistical Office.

Table 8.4
Money supply and credit granted by banks to the non-financial sector in Poland 1989-94
(% increase on year earlier)

Item	1989	1990	1991	1992	1993	1994[b]
Money supply[a]	190.5	396.3	64.8	57.3	28.8	21.5
Credit supply	176.0	253.2	64.4	28.5	33.4	14.0

Note:
[a]   M2 foreign currency accounts excluded.
[b]   As of August.
Source: National Bank of Poland.

At that time, it turned out that banks (not only state-owned but also the newly established) granted credits in a passive way, following the socialist economy pattern, without checking the credit-worthiness of potential borrowers, often making loans with no real collateral. At the same time, just as in the socialist economy era, the demand of non-financial agents, mostly state-owned enterprises, for bank credits was heavy, almost regardless of interest rates. Consequently, the supply of money and credit grew rapidly in 1990 despite the stabilization program.

In the first half of 1990 the central bank hoped to arrest this trend by means of orthodox money supply control instruments. In July the NBP even introduced a type of open-market operations using NBP money bills (for details see Polański, 1994b). Nevertheless, money and credit supply growth was brought under some control only after an old instrument dating back to the socialist economy times was restored. By the autumn of 1990 the Bank resorted to credit ceilings to regulate the supply of bank lending. Thanks to this credit rationing, the growth rate of lending and the money supply slowed, although due to foreign transactions and, from 1991, also financing by the banking sector of the state budget deficit money supply growth was still considerable. Taking into account also the fact that inter-enterprise credits (for details see Polański, 1993, 1994a) performed a significant role at that time, it is easy to understand why a high rate of inflation might continue under the stabilization programme.

Then, the credit supply situation began to change. This was due to privatization, including bank privatization, recession and company failures resulting in the deterioration of banks' credit portfolio (see below) and growing economic uncertainty. Indeed in 1992, the actual supply of bank credits for the non-financial sector was below the credit ceiling. Perhaps surprisingly, credit rationing by the central bank in 1990 was replaced in 1992 with a credit rationing by commercial banks themselves. This rationing clearly reduced credit supply growth in the following years. But despite this the money supply continued its uninterrupted growth after 1992 so contributing to a high rate of inflation.

This money supply growth, despite credit rationing by commercial banks was due to state budget deficit financing by the banking sector (both commercial banks and the NBP) as well as the large trade surplus in 1993-94 which, in view of the internal convertibility of the złoty and the system of administered exchange rates[1] resulted directly in growth of the domestic money supply. Because of underdeveloped financial markets, the NBP and commercial banks had to be the main source of budget deficit financing. On the other hand, the underdevelopment of financial markets made it difficult for the central bank to sterilize the impact of the foreign trade sector on the money supply.

Due to the uneven development of the money market the scope for open market operations, introduced by the NBP on a larger scale from 1993, as an intervention measure was limited. In fact the direct regulation of interest rates remains the basic instrument of central bank intervention in the economy. Theoretically, commercial banks are free to set their own interest rates, however, in practice actual interest rates reflect the direct dependence of most Polish banks on the state (quite simply most are state-owned, for more details see Polański 1994b). More precisely, interest rates on the interbank market are determined purely by market forces, that is, by demand and supply. This, however, is not the case with credits for non-financial agents, the interest rates on which are largely administered. The fact that two different interest rate mechanisms exist side by side reflects the deep segmentation of Polish financial markets.

This overview of the policy pursued by the Polish central bank in the early 1990s suggests that the financial system failed to create an effective and stable framework for policy to be consistent. The poor efficiency of the Polish financial system, reflected in its inadequacy as a channel of transmission for central bank policies meant that the system did not generally operate in the manner typical of market economies.

Capital functions

Although financial systems in the socialist economies had clear monetary functions they performed no capital functions. The essence of these lies in the stimulation and accumulation of savings and in providing economic agents with investable funds. In the socialist system the financial institutions were not intermediaries in the traditional sense of the word: deposits accumulated by banks did not determine their credit-granting activity. Decisions on the volume and structure of credits were taken outside the banking system by the central planning authorities.

As in any other economy, banks operating under the socialist system *did* accumulate savings. Although this was done in a rather passive way (there were no incentives for them to develop this activity), their function was in this respect similar to that performed by banks in market systems. But the banks' role in funds allocation was quite different. As key decisions were traditionally made by the central authorities state-owned banks (and often also new predominantly private banks) entered the 1990s with no experience in risk assessment. Consequently, they were unable to allocate their assets efficiently and this was reflected in the accumulation of "bad loans" (that is, non-performing assets).

Table 8.5
Bad loans in Poland 1991-94
(per cent shares)

Item	1991[a]	1991	1992	1993	1994[b]
As share of bank credits granted to enterprises	8.3	16.2	31.4	33.1	34.1
As share of banks' assets	.	6.7	10.8	10.2	10.1
As share of GDP	1.5	3.7	6.2	6.0	5.2[c]

Note:
[a]   As of June
[b]   As of August
[c]   The ratio takes into account the official forecast of 1994 GDP.
Source: National Bank of Poland and Polish Central Statistical Office.

Bad loans are associated with a number of causes, their significance in the Poland of the 1990s, changing over time. In 1990 and 1991, the emergence of non-performing assets was largely due to the wrong allocation of credit by the central administration in the socialist era and the legacy of bank-enterprise links established in that period. This tight relationship between banks and enterprises encouraged the continued flow of credit to enable repayment of old debts. To have behaved differently would have posed a threat of debtors' bankruptcy, involving even higher costs for the banks. The other major causes of bad loans included high nominal interest rates (see Table 8.3), the disintegration of the Comecon market leading to the insolvency of many exporting companies virtually overnight, as well as the policy induced recession.

The data in Table 8.5 suggest however that the bad loans problem clearly became more apparent after 1991 and remained significant over 1992-94 despite steps to solve this problem. In February 1993, parliament passed an important law on the financial restructuring of enterprises and banks, intended to solve the problem of bad loans connected with credits granted before 1992. The measures introduced by this law were generally helpful (see Pawlowicz's contribution to this volume also Kawalec, Sikora and Rymaszewski, 1994) but the non-performing assets of the banking sector as a whole remained at a high level. In July 1993 they reached their peak as share of bank credits granted (37 per cent), then fell but rose again in 1994 (see Table 8.5).

This suggests that the inadequate allocative ability of banks is largely responsible for bad loans. The Polish banking sector still faces serious problems in evaluating credit worthiness. This is largely due to the fact, already noted, that, in the socialist economy banks did not have to assess the risk involved in granting credits. Moreover, many market economy institutions assisting creditors in risk evaluation (for example, credit information agencies) did not exist in Poland, and legal regulations concerning bankruptcy are far from perfect.

What is the impact of the allocative inadequacy of the Polish financial system on the country's economy? The banks, aware of the difficulties with proper credit allocation, to a large extent simply rationed credit. This was facilitated by allowing banks the opportunity to invest their assets in high yielding state treasury securities issued to finance the budget deficit.

As the banks' slowed credit-granting activity this led to a slow-down in credit supply growth, resulting in falling shares of bad loans in banks' assets and in GDP. However, the share of bad loans in the volume of credits granted did not decline. Thus credit rationing by banks reduced their risk exposure but failed to improve the allocative efficiency of their loan-granting activity.

These features of the Polish banking sector in 1990-94 had broad economy-wide implications. Errors in credit allocation by banks dented the efficiency-oriented pressure of the new economic policy, as enterprises were on many occasions granted credits for further activity despite their lack of genuine economic prospects. For many firms this situation, especially in the early 1990s when credits were still widely available, meant the continuation of "soft-budget" financing typical of the socialist economy. However, the most adverse result of the poor allocative capacity of Polish financial institutions is their considerably limited impact on the selection process, which, in the long run, determines the development of any economy (see Murrell, 1992, on this interpretation of Schumpeterian theory). Central planning has ended but the Polish economy does not yet have an efficient internal financial mechanism able to stimulate sustained economic growth.

Control functions

The control functions of the financial system in a market economy flow from its allocative functions. The institution making available funds to a company or investing them in its equity usually wants to influence the company's decisions. Consequently the financial system in the market economy monitors and disciplines company managers and in some cases also company owners (Rybczyński, 1992, p. 254).

Of course, since the financial system in the socialist economy did not fulfil allocative tasks it could hardly perform control functions. And, as we have noted, the Polish financial system in the early 1990s was not in a position efficiently to exercise control functions. If banks cannot make their customers repay debts or even interest then no-one can expect them to influence the internal activities of their "customers". Moreover, if the supervising and disciplining role of the bank is to bring socially desirable results, these institutions must have access to information on the economy and must be able to predict future economic developments in a way allowing them to make sensible decisions. In this respect, they have to be well in front of the agents that they are supposed to monitor and discipline. But the banks are not in front and six years after the demise of the mono-bank Polish financial institutions in fact do not yet perform these tasks.

Although widely discussed (see for example Carbide and Macer, 1991) the issue of optimal capital allocation and control in a post-socialist economy was not solved by the mid 1990s either in theory or in practice. Should the financial systems of post-socialist countries be more bank-based, with these institutions playing the key role in allocating funds and controlling companies, or should this role be played by the securities market, as in the so-called Anglo-Saxon model? Polish policy here is not clearly defined. The 1989 Banking Act, by advocating universal banking rather pointed to a bank-based financial system. On the other hand, however, privatization has tended to emphasise the role of the securities market as an important channel of supplying companies with capital and a mechanism of control exercised over these companies by their shareholders[2].

Despite the diminished role of bank credits in financing the activities of economic agents in the 1990s, banks are still important institutions in the Polish financial system. It seems that the new financial system developing in Poland will remain bank-based for a considerable time. However new privatization techniques (most notably mass privatization with the creation of new active investment funds) may enhance the role of the securities market and financial system in performing control functions in Poland.

The financial system and Poland's economic development

Despite dramatic changes in the structure of the Polish financial system in the early 1990s, it did not and could not play a major role in the development of the Polish economy over this period. To be sure, the dismantling of the extremely centralized financial system typical of the socialist economy, together with liberalization, added to the system's flexibility, and must have played a positive role in economic restructuring but a closer examination of the Polish financial system shows that it did not make a major contribution to the efficiency of economic policy measures.

First, the highly inadequate financial system and the rapid change in commercial banks' attitudes (the move from a highly passive credit policy to credit rationing) did not provide a stable framework for the central bank. The changing nature of the financial system rendered the conduct of monetary policy very difficult.

Second, the analysis of monetary functions performed by the Polish financial system provides some explanation for the limited success in checking inflation in Poland. In 1990-91 the expansive credit policy of commercial banks was the main reason for laxness in monetary policy while in later years the underdevelopment of financial markets made it necessary for the banking sector to finance the state budget deficit, and this of course was pro-inflationary. At the same time, this underdevelopment created difficulties in eliminating the impact of foreign settlements on money supply growth. Consequently, throughout this period major difficulties with monetary control existed and inflation, despite gradual falling, remained high.

Problems with capital and control functions meant that the poor allocative abilities of Polish banks still allowed "soft budget" financing. Meanwhile credit rationing gave only a limited role to banks in restructuring the Polish economy.

It is evident that the economic recovery recorded in Poland since 1992 is not attributable to a more efficient financial system. Polish growth is largely due to factors outside the financial system (for more on these factors see the paper by Gronicki and Wyżnikiewicz also included in this volume).

Final considerations

Many of the problems presented in this study are visible not only in Poland but also in other post-socialist countries (for example, difficulties concerning money supply control, bad loans, corporate governance issues - see for instance Dittus, 1994). They emerge because transformation has an institutional aspect and institutional change is a slow process. Government decisions may obviously speed up the pace of institutional development but the room for manoeuvre is fairly limited. The experience of Poland and other post-socialist countries in the 1990s shows that the development of a market-type financial system able efficiently to perform its basic functions is bound to take a long time.

While in 1989-93 the decisions of Solidarity governments in Poland were clearly aimed at speeding up systemic changes, reflected in initial changes to the country's financial system, from the re-emergence of a "post-communist" government in September 1993 things may have changed somewhat. Rapid reform may no longer be the case. Some decisions taken by the government that took power in autumn 1993 testify to a slowing of the process of market-oriented transformation. This will have practical implications for the financial system and the evolution towards a market-type system able to perform smoothly monetary, capital and control functions may be delayed. Consequently, the Polish financial system will not be in a position to stimulate economic recovery if and when the other factors (outside the financial system such as exports) contributing to the revival of the economy became exhausted. Therefore, if financial system developments slow they may soon adversely affect the overall rate of economic growth in Poland.

Notes

1 From January 1990 to autumn 1991 Poland had a fixed exchange rate regime, while the crawling-peg exchange rate regime has been in force since the end of 1991.
2 The Warsaw stock exchange was launched quickly (it was functioning by April 1991) and the mass media and politicians attached to it great significance, at least in its early phase.

References

Blommenstein, H.J. and Spencer M.G. (1994), "The Role of Financial Institutions in the Transition to a Market Economy", in Caprio, G., Folkerts-Landau, D., and Lane, T.D., (eds.), *Building Sound Finance in Emerging Market Economies*, International Monetary Fund/World Bank.

Bukharin, N.I. and Preobrazhensky, E. (1974), "The ABC of Communism", in *Socialist Economics Selected Readings*, Nove, A. and Nuti, D.M. (eds.), (Penguin Books, Bungay).

Carbide, J. and Macer C. (1991), "Financial Reform in Eastern Europe: Progress with the Wrong Model", *Oxford Review of Economic Policy*, No. 4.

Díaz-Alejandro, C. (1985), "Good-bye Financial Repression, Hello Financial Crash," *Journal of Development Economics*, vol. XIX.

Dittus, P. (1994), *Corporate Governance in Central Europe: The Role of Banks*, Bank for International Settlements, Basle.

Kawalec, S., Sikora S. and Rymaszewski P. (1994), "Dealing with Bad Debts: The Case of Poland", in Caprio G., Folkerts-Landau, D. and Lane, T.D., (eds.), *Building Sound Finance in Emerging Market Economies*, International Monetary Fund/World Bank.

Kloc, K. (1993), "Ogólna charakterystyka systemu bankowego w Polsce i dynamika jego zmian", (General description of the Polish banking system and its evolution), in Boguszewski P., Federowicz, M., Kloc K., Mizielińska, W., and Smuga, T., *Banki a przedsiębiorstwa (badania empiryczne)* (Banks and enterprises (empirical studies)), The Gdańsk Institute for Market Economics, Transformation of the Economy, vol. 37, Warsaw-Gdańsk.

Murrell, P. (1992), "Evolution in Economics and in the Economic Reform of Centrally Planned Economies", in Clague, C. and Rausser, G.C., (eds.), *The Emergence of Market Economies in Eastern Europe*, (Blackwell, Oxford).

Polański, Z. (1991), "Inflation and the Monetary System in Poland in the 1980s, and the Stabilization Programme 1990," *Osteuropa-Wirtschaft* No. 4.

Polański, Z. (1993), *Polityka kredytowo-pieniężna a system finansowy w Polsce w latach 1990-1993* (Credit-monetary policy and the financial system in Poland 1990-1993), Narodowy Bank Polski, Materiały i Studia nr 40, Warszawa [An English translation to be published in *Russian and East European Finance and Trade*, September-October 1994.]

Polański, Z. (1994a), *Building a Monetary Economy in Poland in the 1990s*, Narodowy Bank Polski, Paper No. 9.

Polański, Z. (1994b), *The Money Market and the Central Bank's Policy in Poland*, The Gdańsk Institute for Market Economics, Transformation of the Economy, vol. 45, Warsaw.

Polański, Z. (1995), *Pieniądz i system finansowy w Polsce. Lata 1982-1993. Przemiana ustrojowa* (Poland's Money and Financial System in Transition: 1982-1993), Wydawnictwo Naukowe PWN.

Rybczyński, T.M. (1992), "The role of finance in the restructuring of resource allocation in Eastern Europe", in Steinherr, A. (ed.), *The New European Financial Market Place* Longman, London and New York.

9 Transformation of the banking system in Poland

Leszek Pawłowicz

Evolution of the Polish banking system

Basic reforms since 1989

In the Polish economy banks play a dominant role on the financial market. The banking system is often heavily criticized. The results of many analyses and surveys show that politicians, journalists and members of the government have a poor view of Polish banks. They accuse banks of overcautious lending and for making collateral requirements that are too demanding. Banking staff are often accused of corruption and incompetence. The popular view is that because of this Poland is not fully utilising available foreign credit lines. The underdevelopment of the Polish financial system is considered by many to be a major obstacle to economic transformation and development. These views, of course, contain elements both of emotion and of truth.

Polish banking reform is extremely difficult not only because of technical backwardness but mainly due to personnel reasons. The bank in the centrally planned economy was an administrative agency and had almost no common features with any commercial bank. Money was an accounting tool only and the central planner decided on capital allocation and production levels. Money required to fulfil output goals was automatically transferred between economic agents. State enterprises did not concentrate any effort on financing their activities since finance and monetary wealth was not decisive in their functioning and development. The most important thing was how much of the country's resources the enterprise could get. Notions of creditworthiness and credit risk were practically nonexistent because the state bank lent money to state enterprises which could not go bankrupt. The existence of the monobank - the National Bank of Poland (NBP) - was enough to achieve this passive function of money and a banking system with independent and different financial institutions was simple unnecessary.

Major banking reform which resulted in a total reconstruction of the Polish banking system took place in 1989. New regulations aimed at establishing market rules in the banking system were introduced. The most important of the new bank regulations, defining the legal status of banks in Poland were:

the banking law of 31 January 1989;
the central bank charter of 31 January 1989;
the foreign currency regulations of 15 February 1989.

The Polish banking law was based on the German model. The regulations enabled a fast transition to the market economy and initiated a process of establishing commercial banks in Poland. Many regulations used Western banking standards as required by agreements signed with the EU.

In 1989 the first significant step towards demonopolization of the banking system was taken. Nine state owned commercial banks were established. They took over deposit and credit activities from the NBP. New banks were created on the base of the forty odd regional branches of the NBP. The underdevelopment of Polish telecommunications was one rationale behind this. However, each of the nine banks had some branches in other banks' areas. This was intended to encourage competition. Banks were no longer subservient to any administrative body and enterprises had not only a formal but also a real opportunity to choose their bank.

The banking law generated very liberal regulations in creating new mainly private banks. The NBP could issue a license if the following simple conditions were fulfilled:

domestic banks had a capital base of $2 million and banks with foreign capital participation a base of $6 million;
the NBP was given a list of given founders together with the bank's charter;
a plan of activities for the first year and the following three years, with forecast of the balance sheet for this period were submitted;
a proper physical establishment existed;

management was in the hands of people with adequate education and experience and without any criminal record.

These liberal regulations resulted in a fast growth of banks in Poland. At the end of 1990 75 banks with nation-wide activities existed, 30 of which were private. The NBP gave several licenses to banks with foreign capital participation. After 1991, the regulations became more restrictive as many private and co-operative banks were close to bankruptcy endangering the stability of financial system.

In the middle of 1994 the ownership structure of the Polish banking system was as follows:

commercial banks (except co-operative banks)	**86**
state owned banks (NBP, PKO BP)	**2**
owned by the treasury	**7**
co-operative bank with state shares	
(Bank Gospodarstwa Krajowego)	**1**
corporations:	**76**
including branches of foreign banks	**3**
co-operative banks	**1,650**
representatives of foreign banks in Poland	**22**

The NBP at last became *the* central bank. According to article 6 of the NBP charter it was to be the central bank in Poland, the bank of issue and the bank of banks. The most important activity of the NBP was to strengthen the Polish złoty.

The major tasks of the NBP are (see Wyczański, 1993):

to manage monetary and foreign exchange policies;
to control the Polish banking system;
to license bank activities;
to grant foreign exchange permits.

The independence of the NBP is secured by the way the governor is nominated. First, the President suggests a name to the Polish sejm which then makes an appointment for a six year period. This term is almost twice as long as parliament's. The governorship may change only through resignation, illness, criminal conviction or as the result of a ruling by the constitutional tribunal.

The creation of a two-tier banking system with independent NBP had a significant impact on the success of the first stage of transition of the Polish economy. The transition started with a stabilization programme agreed upon with the IMF. Changes in monetary, fiscal and income policies constituted the major part of this programme. The most important goal, however, was elimination of hyperinflation and restoration of economic equilibrium. The monetary policy of the NBP was a major tool in achieving this. Monetary policy meant control over the money supply, maintaining positive real interest rates, the introduction of internal convertibility of the Polish złoty and setting a uniform and fixed exchange rate for the złoty against the $US.

The idea of making the Polish złoty internally convertible was innovative and risky. The złoty remained inconvertible according to international standards but the number of foreign currency limitations was extremely small and was comparable to fully convertible currencies (see Pietrzak, 1994). The NBP's monetary policy helped very efficiently to dampen inflation in 1990. The effects in 1993 an 1994 were, however, much smaller.

The monetary instruments used by the NBP gradually became adapted to market economy requirements. The NBP withdrew from administrative regulations and moved to the usual market instruments. Obligatory reserves remained the basic instruments for controlling money supply.

Control over efficient use of financial resources is another important function of the Polish central bank. In 1990, a general inspectorate of banking supervision was created within the NBP. It can ask the governor of the NBP to revoke any bank's license. Since 1992, it has had a significant influence on the stability of the Polish banking system monitoring, among others, how banks observe the NBP's safety rules. By 1995 those rules were similar to those in the EU.

Banks are obliged, according to central bank regulation, to classify credits into four categories: good credits, substandard credits, uncertain credits and lost credits. Banks must set a 100 per cent reserve against lost credits (that is, credits of risk group IV); 50 per cent reserves against uncertain credits (belonging to risk group III) and 20 per cent reserves against substandard credits (the risk group II). There is no need to create any special reserve against good credits. Polish regulations (which are similar to those of the EU) also insist that the Cook solvency ratio (the ratio of bank capital to risk weighted assets) shall not surpass 8 per cent.

Two other features worth mentioning. First, the law on the guarantee fund to be implemented from 1995. This fund will guarantee personal and firms' deposits upto ECU 3,000. Second, new regulations aimed at the financial restructuring of enterprises and banks will have a tremendous impact on the stability and efficiency of the Polish banking system (see also section 3 of this chapter)[1].

This fund will guarantee personal and firms' deposits up to ECU 3,000.[2]

The financial potential of the Polish banking system

The financial assets of the Polish banking system are minor compared to banks' financial assets in developed Western economies. The largest Polish banks have assets valued at about $1.5 billion. Bank Handlowy SA in Warsaw, the largest bank in Central Europe (with respect to capital base), has assets of $3.5 billion. Compared to the largest German, Swiss or Dutch banks they are quite insignificant but in Central Europe Polish banks are considered to be the strongest. Seventeen Polish banks appeared in a recent *Banker* magazine listing of the top 100 banks in Central Europe (see *Nowa Europa*, 27 September 1994) and among the leading 25 there are seven Polish banks (see Table 9.1).

Table 9.1
The largest banks in Central Europe

Banks	Capital $ millions	Assets $ millions
Bank Handlowy SA (BH SA) in Warsaw	**584**	**3,499**
Bulgarian Foreign Trade Bank - Bulgaria	428	16,248
Privredna Bank Zagreb - Croatia	403	2,612
Komercni Banka - Czech Republic	402	9,186
Ceskoslovenska Obchodni Banka - Czech Republic	364	4,260
Ceska Sporitelna - Czech Republic	333	10,462
Powszechna Kasa Oszczednosci BP (PKO BP)	**310**	**6,090**
Vseobecna Uverova Banka - Slovakia	298	4,146
Zagrebacka Banka - Croatia	284	1,962
Konsolidacni Banka Praha - Czech Republic	231	2,982
Orszagos Takarekpentzar Bank - Hungary	228	8,218
Investicni a Postavni Banka - Czech Republic	210	4,142
Bank of Economic Projects - Bulgaria	207	1,357
Bank Gospodarki Żywnościowej (BGŻ)	**178**	**3,246**
Slovenska Sporitelna	171	3,989
Bank Pekao SA	**165**	**6,278**
Bank Gdański	**163**	**1,039**
Banca Romana De Comert Exterior - Romania	160	1,564
Magyar Kulkereskedelmi Bank - Hungary	136	2,026
Stopanska Banka - Macedonia	120	1,465
Bank Przemysłowo-Handlowy	**115**	**1,586**
Banca Agricola - Romania	113	1,803
Romanian Commercial Bank - Romania	104	1,468
National Saving Bank - Bulgaria	104	3,384
Powszechny Bank Kredytowy	**99**	**1,876**

Source: Nowa Europa, 27 September 1994

The level of economic development and size of the banking system are interrelated. If Poland can strengthen macroeconomic stability then the share of banking assets in GDP will grow. Currently this share is one of the lowest in Europe.

Figure 9.1
Share of banking assets in GDP (%)

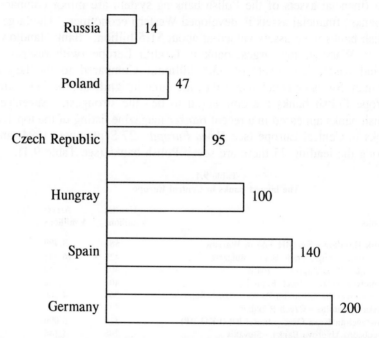

Source: McKinsey Analysis - Seminar paper - Zakopane, 25-27 February 1994

The net assets of Polish banks in 1993 amounted to złoty 860,955 billion and they increased by 6 per cent in real terms compared to 1992 (using the GDP deflator). The liabilities of the non-financial sector form the largest part of bank assets (32.4 per cent in 1994). However, this position is diminishing rapidly. Equities are in second place and their share is growing very fast; in 1992 it was 23 per cent and in the middle of 1994 it reached 24.3 per cent. The deposits of the non-financial sector are the largest part of Polish banks liabilities (56.3 per cent in the middle of 1994, of which about 70 per cent are households' deposits).

The share of bad credits, which was growing very fast until 1992, stabilized thereafter (see Table 9.2).

Table 9.2
Share of "bad loans" in Polish banks credit portfolio

Date (end year)	1991	1992	1993	1994[a]
Credit portfolio (złoty billion)	186,354	222,583	274,979	292,448
Credits from III & IV risk groups[b]	30,497	70,586	93,021	99,987
Share (%)	16.4	31.7	33.8	31.2

Notes:
[a] End March
[b] risk groups are defined as follows, I represents "good" loans, II represents "substandard" loans, III represents "uncertain" loans and IV represents "lost" loans.
Source: Research and analysis department, NBP

The stabilization of bad credits in the total credit portfolio was due to intensive debt restructuring in the seven treasury owned commercial banks (which were re-capitalized over 1993-94). In other banks, the structure of the credit portfolio continued to worsen. This was especially so in co-operative banks. In these banks financial conditions continuously deteriorated as special reserves were created to cover bad loans. The whole banking system (including co-operative banks) reported losses in 1993 and in the first half of 1994. In the first half of 1994 60 commercial banks reported positive gross profits while losses were reported by 26 banks. Of course. the financial standing of banks remains highly varied. The nine treasury commercial banks (two of which have since been privatized) created from the former state mono-bank, are in the best condition. Their average profitability rate was over 15 per cent and four of them had a profitability rate of more than 35 per cent. The worst results were reported by co-operative banks.

The low profitability of the Polish banking system is closely correlated with its worsening credit portfolio and the creation of special reserves necessary for the security of the whole financial system. Those reserves reached złoty 76,761 billion in 1994 and were close to NBP requirements. The structure of reserves shows that several commercial banks created reserves above than minimal requirements but at the end of June 1994 21 banks could not reach the mandatory 8 per cent solvency ratio. This was also due to the low level of banks' capital. In 22 banks the capital base was below złoty 70 billion.

All of this means that the Polish banking system remains stable and operates prudently but only at increasing cost. In the fast growing Polish economy the banking system does not exhibit growing profitability and efficiency. The relatively small potential of Polish banks is used inefficiently.

The credit market

Improvement in the capital allocation mechanism is crucial for the further development of the Polish economy. But better capital allocation depends on the banking system, especially on the credit market, and the efficient transformation of savings into investment.

In a fast growing Polish economy demand for credit should increase. McKinsey, for example, expect the real value of credits to grow faster than GDP. Developments in the Polish economy however buck this trend. It is true that the banks' real net assets increased in 1993 by 6 per cent but the real value of credits extended to enterprises fell by 4 per cent. This growth in assets was possible due to the flow of restructuring bonds issued by the treasury. But the only really rapid growth was in bad credits. They increased nominally by 62 per cent and in real terms by 25 per cent (see *Banki*, 1993). Thus limited growth in lending coincided with a worsening of the credit portfolio.

In the forecast published by J. Rajski and Z. Szpringer (in *Banki* 1993) it was expected that the share of the liabilities of the non-financial sector in bank assets would decrease in 1994. The role of the credit market looked likely to diminish further.

The falling share of bank lending in financing economic growth may be due either to limited demand or to supply restrictions. It is certainly the outcome of the interplay of lender and borrower behaviour. The latter usually seeks the cheapest source of financing and this changes the structure of the borrower's liabilities. The former seeks the most profitable and safest investment and this changes the structure of the lender's assets.

At the beginning of the 1990s in most of the OECD countries credit expansion slowed. The relevant literature discusses whether this tendency was due to recession or was a more permanent phenomenon. A lower demand for credits may be caused by the availability of other sources of financing. The capital market is the major alternative source of finance for enterprises. In this situation, commercial banks try to become an intermediary in acquiring financial resources on the capital market. This activity is another source of profit for banks and is less risky than lending directly.

The Polish capital market is developing at a fast pace but it is still weak. From 1994 corporations listed on the Warsaw stock exchange more frequently issued shares to raise additional capital. Sales of other securities (bonds and similar instruments) is limited, mainly due to the need to secure a return in competition with government bonds which guarantee a high real interest rate. In Poland, there are no alternatives to borrowing as a source of finance. This means that financial intermediaries other than banks are unlikely to play a significant role in the allocation of capital in the near future.

On the supply side of the credit market banks must achieve relatively higher profitability. Profitability depends in part on the cost of lending. It is worth considering to what extent credit costs depend on the bank alone and what opportunities the bank has to reduce lending costs. The most important factor is the quality of the credit portfolio. It is higher when the share of non-performing assets is small and this depends in turn on borrowers' standing. However, the majority of Polish enterprises are in a state of permanent crisis regardless of the (since 1993) booming economy. The characteristic feature of Polish enterprises is difficulty in adapting to new market conditions. The major factors responsible for the crisis in the enterprise sector were:

1 the collapse of the Soviet Union;
2 the liberalization of Polish foreign trade in 1989 which generated strong import competition, but, at the same time a significant increase of exports to the West was hard to achieve due to technological backwardness and weak management not able to work in a competitive environment or overcome Western protectionism; Western markets happened to be more hermetic than was expected;
3 the domestic "shock therapy" which insisted on real positive interest rates in order to fight hyperinflation.

At the beginning of 1990, interest rates reached 60 per cent monthly and enterprises with large debts were especially adversely affected. In a very short period they became uncreditworthy and they often stopped servicing debts to banks, suppliers and the exchequer. Banks, in turn, added penalty interest or rolled over credits. Soon, enterprises fell into a debt trap. The deterioration of enterprise liquidity also resulted in the growth of inter-enterprise debt. In this situation, those enterprises which were not in the debt trap were affected by inter-enterprise debts regardless of their better solvency levels. A growing number of payment obligations were paid irregularly and many of them became "doubtful".

The crisis in the enterprise sector was reflected in banks' credit portfolios, where non-performing liabilities were growing. A deteriorizing credit portfolio was the most significant cause of too restrictive lending. In a certain sense banks were responsible for deepening enterprise indebtedness. This crisis, with some delay, then transferred itself to the banks. The only possible solution was a radical debt restructuring. The device for achieving this in Poland was to be the general privatization programme. It aimed at increasing the efficiency of several hundred enterprises by distributing them between newly created investment funds which would then restructure the firms concerned. The domestic and foreign capital and experience available to these funds could, it was thought, offset negative effects of "shock therapy". The National Investment Funds (*Narodowe Fundusze Inwestyjce - NFI*)[3] together with the programme for restructuring enterprise debt managed by the banks would, the authors of the programme hoped, positively influence the Polish economy. The banking environment would be hit less hard by the enterprise crisis. However, delays in implementing this privatization programme also had a significant impact in delaying the improvement of the banks' credit portfolio. A programme of financial restructuring of enterprises in the absence of the *further* restructuring support from the *NFI*, simply diminishes and slows the overall benefit to the economy. It was expected that this restructuring programme would create the base for a future rational allocation of capital through the credit market. This effect, however, would not be immediate.

Economic restructuring is being carried out with no co-ordination between the ministries of finance, privatization or the NBP. It is also moving at a relatively slow pace. This means that the credit portfolio is still deteriorating. The intensity of this deterioration is least severe in the nine commercial banks created from the mono-bank in 1989 and in banks with foreign capital. It is greatest in co-operative banks and also in the six from the largest 15 banks (excluding the nine commercial banks mentioned above).

A cumulation of "bad debts" creates dangers for the stability of the entire banking system. In 88 commercial banks deposits are not guaranteed by the state. Some of these banks could soon be bankrupt. In 1993, according to NBP estimates, seven banks with 70 branches and złoty 6 trillion in deposits were endangered. Twenty one commercial banks made losses in 1994 and in fifteen the solvency ratio was negative. A similar situation exists in 80 to 100 co-operative banks (in these banks deposits are guaranteed by the state and clients can lose only interest).

In this situation, the NBP implemented radical measures aimed at creating safety norms. These include a minimal level of bank capital, obligatory creation of special reserves (related to "bad debts") and establishing the solvency ratio. However, these have been in place only for a short period and lack of cohesion with the tax system increases credit costs. Most of the special reserves were not tax deductible. Moreover banks have to pay profits tax on them (at 40 per cent) and this raised considerably the cost of implementing the safety regulations.

The high level of obligatory reserves also has a significant impact on credit costs. A very high level of obligatory reserves (23 per cent for current deposits and 10 per cent for time deposits) - one of the highest in the world - is justified by overliquidity on the interbank market and an underdeveloped money market unable to transmit the monetary policy of the NBP. These high reserves ratios increase credit costs and are responsible for the large spread between interest on deposits and credits. From September 1992 to the time of writing in late 1994 these ratios were not changed. It seems, however, that even with excess supply on the inter-bank market the ratios should be gradually lowered. If not, the high costs of financial intermediation will adversely influence credit activities.

Summing up, the following factors are responsible for high credit costs in the Polish banking system:

1 The structural crisis of many state-owned enterprises leading to a low quality credit portfolio;
2 The relatively slow pace of the programme for financial restructuring of enterprises caused mainly by delays in implementing the mass privatization programme;
3 The very rapid implementation by the NBP of safety procedures;
4 A tax system which does not ease the introduction of the safety regulations introduced by the NBP;
5 Too high levels of obligatory reserves.

Lending is becoming less profitable and this clearly influences credit supply.

The profits structure of Polish banks is quite different from that observed in the West. Lending is a very high risk activity. In these conditions, the tendency to limit and discriminate credits is rational. Credits are usually provided to firms from only the best rated, I and II credit risk groups, for short terms only. The general financial condition of enterprises does not suggest that the number of creditworthy borrowers will increase in the near future.

The price of credit is becoming crucial in this situation. In 1994 banks with other sources of revenue asked creditworthy borrowers to pay interest at a rate of about 35 per cent, and from slightly more risky customers they usually asked for over 40 per cent. These high rates together with the poor performance of enterprises (only 25 per cent of firms reported profitability of more than 10 per cent in 1994) create a barrier to the efficient use of credits and for some borrowers it deepens the debt trap. It forces a mutual self-financing across the majority of enterprises and increases the value of inter-enterprise debts. Credit channels are becoming blocked despite the low indebtedness of Polish enterprises which, measured as a ratio of debt to capital, ranged in 1993 from 7.3 to 29.3 per cent (and averaged 16.1 per cent) (see *Banki* 1993).

This relatively high cost of borrowing is a crucial barrier in financing economic development. It limits investment credits, which itself is dangerous as the investment ratio is between 19 to 21 per cent of GDP. Statistical investigations suggest that there is a significant relationship between the structure of banks' loans portfolio and the value of investment credits. Usually high, but negative, correlation coefficients are reported between "irregular" portfolios and investment credits. Banks' involvement in financing investments depends on the quality of their assets.

The low level of investment stems from relatively high interest rates on borrowing and low enterprise profitability. The share of bank loans in financing investment in Poland is around 29 to 30 per cent, whereas in Germany 36 to 42 per cent is more typical.

A lower demand for loans from creditworthy enterprises is worrying. In 1993, the share of enterprises which paid off their debts and did not acquire any new loans increased by 17 per cent. This suggests that clients attractive to banks are reluctant to ask for new loans because of the high level of interest rates.

The banks set the price of credits for the best clients at the level of minimal profitability. One can say that this is influenced by monopolistic practices, especially for credits outstanding to small businesses. This not true, however, for economic agents which are creditworthy and attractive to banks. The lower demand for investment funds from these firms is a symptom of the crisis on the credit market in Poland. The efficiency of transforming savings into investment in the Polish banking system is low. Our conclusion is that over the last five years Polish banks have, in general, performed poorly from the wider economic viewpoint.

The financial restructuring of enterprises and commercial banks

The restructuring programme[4]

It is widely acknowledged that a distorted credit market is a major obstacle to the further development of the Polish economy. The interrelation between the structural crisis of enterprises, inter-enterprise debts, the stability of the banking system and distorted lending patterns are becoming ever stronger. In this situation, the implementation of a debt restructuring programme was expected to reverse these negative tendencies. This programme was intended to create new, more sound foundations for a capital allocation mechanism, to lead to lower interest rates and open hitherto blocked credit channels for enterprises.

This debt restructuring programme was designed by the ministry of finance. Its objective was to improve banks' financial standing by reducing the bad debt portfolio, supplying additional capital to some state-owned banks and financial restructuring of banks' debtors.

The improvement of the financial standing of the banking sector was to come from increasing banks' capital while at the same time reducing their financial commitment to uncreditworthy economic agents. The latter was to be done by writing off the debts of borrowers who could not function in the new economic conditions and by renegotiating credit agreements with those borrowers who, according to the banks and other lenders, would eventually be able to pay off outstanding debt. The financial restructuring of such debtors could be done only in those cases where there was a real possibility that they would survive in the new economic setup. Writing off debts, rescheduling debt service obligations and debt-to-equity swaps were the major restructuring instruments envisaged by the restructuring law.

The new regulations envisaged debt reduction through:

1   Bank "conciliatory agreements", applicable only for enterprise in which the treasury owns more than 50 per cent of equity;
2   Public sale of debts.

A bank, on the motion of a debtor and after presenting a proposal of the firm's recovery, could conclude a "conciliatory agreement". In this case, court mediation was not required. The only precondition for concluding this agreement was prior approval of at least 50 per cent of creditors. This 50 per cent then dictate conditions of the conciliatory agreement for other creditors.

The main instruments of the conciliatory agreement included:

debt reduction;
debt-to-equity swaps;
grace period;
conversion of short-term debts into long-term debts.

Any bank concluding such an agreement on behalf other creditors and itself was implicitly responsible for:

evaluation of the restructuring programme;
monitoring of the restructuring programme;
seeking eventual portfolio investors.

A bank which did not believe that debtor recovery was realistic and did not see a possibility of regaining either the whole or part of its claims could decide to sell on its debt with a discount. The only condition was that it had to be a public sale. The sale could be run in three ways: by tender, public offer or negotiations based on public invitation. The restructuring law stresses three significant points:

debtor consent is not required;
bank secrecy law was not binding;
debts could not be sold to the debtor or any of its affiliates.

Any individual creditor holding at least 30 per cent of the overdue claims on a state-owned enterprise, where this enterprise could not pay off its debts in a 30 day period, could convert debt to equity at a very lucrative rate.

Banks included in the restructuring programme were forced to separate "doubtful" or "lost" assets (so called III and IV category assets in NBP regulations) which were in their credit portfolios at the end of 1991 and on the date of enacting the law. The value of assets identified to be restructured (banks had until July 1993 to update this) was a base for calculating the amount of additional capital required by banks. Because of the restructuring bonds which were transferred to banks the solvency ratio in banks included in this programme surpassed 12 per cent.

Simultaneously, banks were asked to establish work-out units (detached from credit departments) responsible for preparing a strategy for debt restructuring. These departments for so-called bad loans were also obliged to take on any other "difficult credits" which were not included in restructuring programme.

Banks had until 31 March 1994 to sell assets (in the case of the BGŻ and PKO BP banks they had until 30 September 1994) where debtors had not fully serviced debts for 3 months, or if debts remained unrestructured, or if debtors went bankrupt, or were liquidated.

This short implementation period forced banks to apply new methods of debt recovery which were not often used before. Conciliation procedures, debt to equity swaps and sales of debts all involved banks in investment banking activities. These activities had a great impact on the enterprise sector. The measure of this impact is not the number of borrowers whose debts were written off, or who went bankrupt, but its success in introducing basic market mechanisms based, often for the first time, on a clear-cut split of property rights between creditor and debtor.

According to the restructuring law banks are creditors with special powers enabling them to negotiate outside court and on behalf of other creditors. The aim of negotiations was to work out restructuring programmes which on the one hand would enable debtors to re-establish their creditworthiness and on the other hand would recover for creditors as much recompense as possible. The result was that many enterprises cleared their debts and restructured their activities. The majority of conciliation agreements also envisaged privatization.

An important outcome of the active role of banks in the restructuring processes was a significant denting in the "claimant" attitude of debtors, so frequent in the past. Only in a few cases did the firm's supervisory board or management or trade unions try to use political pressure through parliament or ministries, and when they did the pressure exerted was rarely successful. The ministry of finance refused to allow any government body to interfere in the debt restructuring activities of the commercial banks. The ministry itself was not an active player in the restructuring process but simply supervised its implementation. Its role was limited to two functions: the general supervision (as owner) of banks and the interpretation of the law for all agents taking part in the restructuring process. The banks had more or less a free hand in debt restructuring and the political protection of debtors, common in the past, was practically eliminated. This attitude forced debtors to use the services of professional advisers on a wide scale. As a result, enterprises demanded more outside professional help with financial analysis in one of the most positive aspects of the restructuring programme.

The banks decided that non-viable enterprises should either be closed or their debts sold. Further access to finance was available only in cases when buyers of debts were potential investors. Otherwise, enterprises were either made bankrupt or liquidated.

The introduction of the rule that the lender had a right to restructure and/or refinance the enterprise together with the ending of administration coercion on lenders was probably the most important effect of the restructuring programme. The programme included mainly the state treasury and units which were either directly or indirectly controlled by the treasury. Thus any financial transfer in this sector was meaningless from the financial point of view (what the treasury loses in the banking system, through debt write-offs it gains when it sells a viable enterprise). It is, however, immensely meaningful from the economic view point if capital becomes reallocated according to rational principles. Research in this area continues and we must wait to see whether the reallocation of capital resulting from the restructuring programme was indeed efficient.

An evaluation of the restructuring programme

The Gdańsk Institute is currently running a research project on the effects of the financial restructuring programme. The objectives of this programme can be summarized as follows. It aimed to:

1   restructure enterprises which look like being able to function in a competitive environment;
2   eliminate inefficient companies either through bankruptcy or sale of debts;
3   limit inter-enterprise debts;
4   create a sound banking system.

The Gdańsk research encompassed the restructuring activities of seven treasury-owned commercial banks which obtained capital injections of złoty 11,000 billion. The first stage of the restructuring programme ended on 31 March 1994. We consider each of the programme's objectives in turn below.

In these commercial banks 17 per cent of the value of difficult credit portfolios consisted of credits given to non-viable enterprises. The rest, that is 83 per cent, was covered by the financial restructuring programme. There was a risk that banks would diffuse and spread too thinly available financial resources. However, our research indicates that banks' decisions were not arbitrary: objective criteria and procedures in risk assessment were used systematically.

Restructuring activities were based on:

bank conciliation procedures covering 80-84 per cent of restructured debts;
court conciliation procedures covering 11-15 per cent of restructured;
civil-legal agreements, covering about 5 per cent of restructured debts.

The bank conciliation procedure was therefore the most frequently used restructuring procedure. For the purpose of our project we selected a sample of 122 such deals covering about złoty 8,000 billion of debts.

Banks started conciliation procedures in June 1993 three months after the debt restructuring law was enacted. On a monthly basis the largest number of conciliations (34 per cent) occurred in December 1993 and the largest number of concluded bank enterprise deals (70 per cent) was, not surprisingly, in March 1994, just before the programme's 31 March deadline. On one hand the short period given to implement the law had some negative effects such as the clogging up of the courts with hearings and a concentration of debt sales. On the other hand it succeeded in mobilizing banks to intensify restructuring activities.

A more detailed description of the bank conciliation deals goes as follows:

72 per cent of enterprises were state-owned, 22 per cent were treasury owned corporations and 6 per cent were joint stock companies;
mostly large and medium size companies were included. The average employment in our sample was about 1,300 employees;
by sector the largest number of bank managed restructuring deals was in light and electro-machinery industries; and
by region the largest number of conciliations were in Jelenia Góra, Opole, Łódź, Wrocław and Wałbrzych provinces.

According to the banks, the bank's own restructuring efforts had the following advantages:

the banks could encourage the debtor to introduce specific restructuring activities;
debts with collateral or mortgage could be included in the programme;
it was possible to conclude a deal when creditors owning 50 per cent of the debt agree, regardless of the number of creditors, so favouring heavily committed lenders;
debts owed to the state treasury could be included in the programme.

These advantages meant that in several cases banks decided to use the bank's own conciliation process despite the court conciliatory proceedings.

On the other hand the major disadvantages from a creditors viewpoint were that:

their financial standing was significantly reduced due to the reduction of the assets base which could, in turn, lead to lower liquidity and in some cases to bankruptcy;
there was no agreement on the value of restructured debts with other creditors;
the creditor had no influence on the conditions and terms agreed;
long debt repayment periods.

Our research shows that the following debt reduction instruments were most frequently used:

write-offs of part of the debt (interest and/or capital);
paying off the debt in quarterly instalments during the three years from the date the agreement with banks was enacted;
immediate paying of the debt;
debt-to-equity swaps.

The major obstacles to successful implementation of the restructuring process were:

lack of a macroeconomic strategy for the Polish economy;
lack of stable financial and fiscal policy;
lack of professional advisers;

the poor connection of the debt restructuring process with the privatization programme and especially the unclear position of the ministry of privatization and ministry of finance in debt-to-equity swaps, as well as the lack of clarity on the competencies of the ministry of privatization in the restructuring process;

lack of co-operation of the ministry of finance and general inspectorate of bank supervision in terms of reporting, the taxation of special reserves and credits for government investment;

lack of reprivatization law and chaos in property rights;

unemployment.

Debt to equity swaps were used in 30 per cent of bank-enterprise debt deals. The survey found why work-out departments decided to use this form of restructuring. In many cases, minimization of restructuring costs was the major reason. Moreover, debt-to-equity swaps gave banks have a greater influence on the enterprise restructuring process.

Our survey found that all banks forecast an improvement in the financial standing of enterprises included in the conciliation process and an increase in value of shares they owned. Banks said they would like to sell these shares to other investors after 2-3 years. Banks also began seeking potential investors. In two banks, the intention was to separate the shares portfolio from bank's assets and transfer them to a newly established firm. One of the banks established a special investment fund which included shares of restructuring enterprises.

Bankruptcy and debt sales

Data gathered in six banks indicated that courts enforced bankruptcy in 162 cases. Banks' losses amounted to złoty 620 billion. One quarter of this sum arose from cases initiated by banks and the rest in cases initiated by boards of enterprises or other creditors.

Our research indicates that 68 per cent of banks' commitments to firms which went bankrupt before 31 March 1994 were in manufacturing enterprises. In this group, enterprises in the light industry had the largest share (27 per cent) with electro-machinery industry (17 per cent) in second place. In the energy sector and metallurgy there were no bankruptcies.

State-owned enterprises accounted for 38 per cent of all bankruptcies. There were no bankruptcies among companies owned by the treasury as in corporate sector.

Banks put on sale the debts of 378 enterprises. The book value of these debts was złoty 2,400 billion. The banks saw two major advantages in debt sales. First, it permitted recovery of larger sums than in the case of bankruptcy (as outstanding obligations to the social security fund and treasury take precedence in the bankruptcy processes). Second, it required relatively small financial resources and was a fast procedure. Our research suggested that banks recovered on average 23 per cent of capital and 12.2 per cent of interest. The price of debt sold was in the range of 8 to 50 per cent of its book value.

The most successful sales (by sector) were in:

manufacturing with 64 debts sold out of 154 put on sale, with the greatest success (sales to debt ratio) in electro-machinery industry (90.9 per cent) and food processing (66.7 per cent);
the co-operative sector with 47 debts were put on sale but 63.8 per cent sold;
the agricultural sector, 56.8 per cent debts sold.

Sales were relatively difficult in:

the trade sector, 144 put on sale debts but only 26.9 per cent sold;
with natural persons, 189 debts put on sale and only 39.5 per cent sold;
the public sector, accounting for 19.5 per cent of the total number of debts put on sale but for 86.3 per cent of all debts by value; the sales/debts ratio was 33.3 per cent.

Limiting inter-enterprise debts

In the first quarter of 1994, the share of overdue payments between firms fell. The largest decrease was observed in the manufacturing sector (about 4 per cent). It is, however, too early to say what the impact of the restructuring process was on inter-enterprise debts. It is possible that after successful completion of all conciliation agreements the share of overdues will decrease further.

Creating a sound banking system

The Gdańsk research indicates that the share of problem credits in the total credit portfolio of investigated commercial banks decreased from 34.8 per cent at the end of 1991 to 32 per cent in the middle of 1994.

The share of credits covered by the restructuring law amounted to 82 per cent of all problem credits (from the base portfolio) set according to the restructuring law). According to the ministry of finance the share of bad loans fell to 10-20 per cent (at 31 March 1994). This seems, however, too optimistic. Nevertheless we have undoubtedly observed some positive tendencies in reducing the share of problem loans.

The investigated banks themselves forecast that at the end of 1994 the share of problem loans would decline to 22.8 per cent and the base portfolio to 15.1 per cent of the total credit portfolio. They also forecast a further decrease in 1995 and 1996. The share of bad loans is expected to reach 7.8 per cent in 1996 (the current level observed in developing countries). This will have a significant impact on credit costs and simultaneously on the general level of interest rates.

The debt restructuring law was viewed by the treasury as a tool for improving the financial standing of banks, increasing their market value and finally, introducing new control mechanisms over the credit portfolio. Banks viewed the law as once-for-all administrative act. This may mean that the restructuring process could slow in the future.

We certainly observed new positive trends in credit management. Several commercial banks adopted Western credit procedures together with detailed classification of credit risks. Another procedure applied by banks was the constant monitoring of normal and sub-standard credits. Early warning systems like these can save banks considerable money. Banks have also intensified spending on the professional training of staff in work-out units. The first stage of the restructuring programme ended on 31 March 1994 but restructuring activities will still go on as the implementation of programmes, the seeking-out of potential investors, and the monitoring and supervising of conciliatory agreements has only begun.

Intensive restructuring activities affected only the six commercial banks separated from the mono-bank, BGŻ and PKO BP. These banks obtained capital injections valued at złoty 21,000 billion. In return they were under the strong administrative supervision of the ministry of finance. Administrative coercion may be efficient in the short term but its role in the future will certainly diminish. In our view there are too few economic pressures to force a permanent restructuring process in enterprises and banks. The tax system is also neutral in this respect. And there is a risk that the positive tendencies observed in credit portfolios could be reversed.

Restructuring activities in other banks are less intensive. Their credit portfolio is deteriorating rapidly. The profitability of these banks is decreasing mainly due to the high reserve ratio required by the NBP.

Too many banks are endangered. If they went bankrupt this would weaken the stability of the Polish banking system. The cost of bail-outs is increasing. Up until 31 July 1994 the NBP had spent złoty 4,500 billion in helping ailing banks.

Recently, a special "lifeboat" fund was proposed (based on an annual fee of 0.4 per cent of risk-weighted assets) with new regulations imminent as 1994 drew to a close. This imposes, however, an additional cost on wealthy banks (which probably will not use the fund's resources) and it will be transferred into an additional increase in credit costs. It will not push banks to improve their credit portfolio and it increases the risk of reversing positive tendencies observed during the recent restructuring process.

The Polish banking system is in crisis. Further successful developments in the financial restructuring of enterprises and banks make introduction of better mechanisms of capital allocation possible. They will also improve the distorted credit market. There are however many uncertainties which prevent a too optimistic forecast.

Notes

1 See also the companion chapter 8 by Polański in this volume.
2 Deposits in banks created before 1989 are fully secured by treasury guarantee whereas deposits in other banks are secured by the NBP up to ECU 3,000. These guarantees are given only to personal deposits and firms are not covered.
3 See Blazyca, chapter 2, p. 15.
4 See also Blazyca, chapter 2, p19 and Polański, chapter 8, p. 131.

References

Banki (1993): Raport na IV Walne Zgromadzenie Związku Banków Polskich, (Banks 1993: Report presented to the fourth general meeting of the Polish banks' association), Warsaw, 1994.

Pietrzak, E., (1994), *Wpływ systemu dewizowo-kursowego wewnętrznej wymienialności złotego na transformację polskiej gospodarki w latach 1990-94*, (The influence of internal złoty convertibility on Polish economic transformation 1990-94), (GIME), Gdańsk.

Wyczański, R., (1993), *Polski system bankowy 1990-1992*, (The Polish banking system 1990-1992), Warsaw.

10   Poland and Europe

Krystyna Gawlikowska-Hueckel

The collapse of the status quo in Europe in 1989 resulted in a change in the European Union's stance towards the countries of the former Soviet Bloc - a fact that was reflected in the signing in 1989 of the *Agreement on Trade and Economic Co-operation*. This agreement, together with the relevant protocol signed between Poland and the European Coal and Steel Community, concluded the period of unregulated trade relations which had lasted since 1975. Later, in 1994, this was replaced by the more far-reaching *Europe Agreement*.[1]

The preamble of the latter includes a statement which is particularly promising for Poland: it recognizes "the fact that the final objective of Poland is to become a member of the Community and that this association in the view of the parties will help to achieve this objective."[2]

The importance of this statement cannot be overestimated, as it is the key to our understanding of the long-term strategy of Polish foreign policy, as well as providing the direction for the overall economic reform-programme in Poland.

In the period of less than a year after the Agreement's coming into effect, the Union's stance vis-a-vis Poland and other associated countries has undergone a further evolution.   The community summit at Copenhagen in June 1993 marked the turning point in this respect, as one historic decision was taken there, namely, the recognition that membership for the associated countries is a shared objective, a declaration which implies that the Community is willing to assist the countries of Central and Eastern Europe in their ambition of joining the

Union.

The basic aim, which is considered as a precondition for the economic integration of Poland, is the convergence of its legal system to that of the European Community. As it was put in the Agreement, "The Contracting parties recognize that the major precondition for Poland's economic integration into the Community is the approximation of that country's existing and future legislation to that of the Community. Poland shall use its best endeavours to ensure that future legislation is compatible with Community legislation" (*Europe Agreement*, Chapter III, art.68-70, p.29). Apart from the adjustment of the legal mechanism itself, a whole range of other reforms is indispensable, reforms aiming at the introduction of new competition rules and the unification of norms and standards as well as macroeconomic policy adjustments.

The achievement of such a wide range of reforms poses a number of challenges for the Polish economy. The costs of transformation connected with the liberalization of trade, with the restrictive monetary policy, as well as with dynamic restructuring are very high in the short run and constitute a considerable burden for a society which is not wealthy. It must be borne in mind that the level of economic development and the standard of living in Poland is much lower than in the countries of the twelve.[3] There is, however, a general awareness in Polish society that the full integration of Poland into the European Union constitutes a historic chance for the country.

This chapter aims to assess the main benefits which are to be gained, as well as the barriers which Poland must overcome on its way to the Community - obstacles which exist on both the Polish and the European sides. We draw here on extensive research carried out by the Gdańsk Institute for Market Economics.

Disparities in regional development: Poland and the European Union

The distance between Poland and the Community can be measured not only in terms of differences in economic structure and the economic regulations in force but also in terms of the standard of living. In January 1994 the average gross wage in the enterprise sector amounted to złoty 4,631,700 (about $200). In 1993 Polish GDP amounted to $1,900 per inhabitant, while the average for the Community was $20,671. For the two least developed members of the Community - Greece and Portugal - the index in question amounts to ECU 6,823 and ECU 8,138 (around $5,686 and $6,782) respectively. On the optimistic assumption that the associated countries will sustain GDP growth at 5 per cent a year, they will succeed in reaching the level of the least wealthy country of the Union after 17 years, so long, however, that the increase in GDP in the least developed member state shall not exceed an annual rate of 2.5 per cent.

The discrepancy between Poland and the Union can also be assessed in terms of the level of industrial development, with Polish industrial potential being considerably inferior as well as technically obsolete. The structure of industry is dominated by traditional branches. Much of GDP is generated by agriculture (6.8 per cent in the case of Poland). It must be noted that the above statistics represent the average figures for Poland as a whole. Unfortunately there are numerous regions in the country with a level of development much lower than the average. The Gdańsk Institute for Market Economics has undertaken long-term studies into Poland's attractiveness for investors on a regional basis. The results of those studies point to the underdevelopment of numerous areas. The best results in industrial development have been achieved by areas that are naturally predisposed towards industry: those endowed with natural resources (upper and lower Silesia) and vovoidships (counties) in which the development of a particular branch of industry has been a continuation of a process which commenced in the nineteenth century (for example the textile industry) or resulted from geographical location (as in the case of shipbuilding). Today, such regions as Warsaw, Katowice, Gdańsk, Poznan, Łódz, Kraków, Szczecin, and Wrocław constitute by far the best developed areas of Poland, ahead of others in practically every respect. Apart from their industrial base they are characterised by a better infrastructure in terms of market, transport and telecommunications, as well as a higher absorptive potential of the market. It is in these areas that the majority of institutions of higher education are situated. It is there that the most dynamic structural and ownership transformations are taking place. Much of the investment with the participation of foreign capital is located in these regions.

The vovoidships which are weaker economically are mainly those in eastern Poland, whose character is predominantly agricultural. In view of the considerable agricultural overmanning in Poland there is an urgent need for profound structural changes and the creation of new workplaces, especially in those regions where manufacturing is based predominantly on agriculture. Here, however, the process of restructuring is confronted with particularly difficult barriers. The areas in question are characterised by a high level of unemployment, a below-average absorptive potential of markets, and a relatively lower level of investment. What is more, they are also neglected in terms of the communication and transport infrastructure. Although industry there is weakly developed, the degree of environmental pollution is very high with degradation of arable land and a forests in a poor state. Despite the proximity of the enormous market in the East, those areas attract the least foreign capital. Consequently, there are good reasons to suspect that regional disparities in Poland may increase.

The division into more or less developed vovoidships is conspicuously asymmetrical, the "better-off" ones being considerably fewer in number. The Gdańsk Institute estimates that some 19 vovoidships may be considered to be "above average" with 30 in the "below average" category. It must also be borne in mind that even the most economically advanced regions of Poland are still backward in comparison with the European average.

It is this disparity in the levels of industrial development that constitutes the main obstacle in Poland's way to the Union and results from the fact that one of the basic objectives of European integration is the lessening of differences in the level of development between member states. The problem of socio-economic cohesion was clearly expressed in the Single European Act. Put explicitly, greater cohesion equals the elimination of the distance between the particular regions. That is being achieved by stimulating economic growth in the least developed areas, so as to remove inter-regional disparities and make it possible for all the countries of the Union to develop in a less uneven way. To achieve this, activities are conducted and financed within the framework of the so-called structural funds as well as through the European Investment Bank by means of other financial instruments.

In order to increase the effectiveness of the structural funds their reform has been instituted. This reform is based on the assumption that they should have five priority objectives. Regions coming under objective one are those whose per capita GDP is below 25 per cent of the Community average; objective two focuses on those whose rates of unemployment are above the Community average; objectives three and four concentrate on the serious issues of long-term unemployment and the occupational integration of young people; objective "five a" deals with the modernization of agricultural production structures; objective "five b" deals with regions that have multiple problems of rural development.

An analysis of the objectives of the structural funds, in the context of the economic situation in Poland, testifies to the fact that Poland qualifies in a clear and unambiguous manner. All the criteria applied to the less developed regions are applicable to Poland. It has been estimated that were the mechanism of cohesion to be applied, the admission to the European Union of Poland, Hungary, the Czech Republic, and Slovakia would cost ECU eight billion, or one third of what has been spent on the less developed regions in the course of 17 years. This fact alone illustrates the scale of the needs of those countries on the one hand, and of the increase in the Union's expenditure on the other. Such a strenuous financing would call either for drastic cuts in expenditure in the member states or a 60 per cent increase in obligatory contributions on the part of those states. The reduction of expenditure within the Union would imply the withdrawal of financial assistance for those who have most relied on structural funds - farmers, above all - which would lead to considerable discontent among these groups.

The *Europe Agreement* and problems of economic structure and competitiveness

The part of the *Europe Agreement* concerning trade (implemented from 1 March 1992) provides for the creation within a period of 10 years of a free trade zone for industrial goods.[4]

The mutual gains are specified in the so-called asymmetry of benefits, which is based on the assumption that it is the Polish side that will derive greater gain from the association. In accordance with this principle Poland embarks on the process of liberalization of trade later than the Community, the aim being to protect the Polish market and partially to soften the shock caused by import competition from the countries of the twelve.[5]

According to the accepted schedule, on 1 March 1993 Poland lowered import duties for 27 per cent of non-agricultural goods from the Community (with respect to prices from 1990). In accordance with the principle of asymmetry the Union removed import duties on approximately 55 per cent of Polish products, while for much of the remaining non-agricultural goods customs duties were reduced by 25-30 per cent.

As has been demonstrated above, Poland enjoys certain privileges guaranteed in the agreement. Their actual scale, however, can be ascertained by means of a more detailed analysis of the commercial turnover between the respective sides. The amount and structure of commercial turnover between Poland and the European Union is of modest proportions. Poland's share in the trade of the Community, calculated in total (that is, intra- plus extra-trade) amounts to a mere 0.5 per cent, while with partners from outside the Union it is 1.5 per cent (by way of example, for the EFTA countries the corresponding figure is 26 per cent).[6] For Poland, however, the Community is the main trading partner.   In 1993, 63.2 per cent of Poland's exports were directed at the European Union market, while imports from that area amounted to 57.2 per cent of the Polish total.[7]

The liberalization of tariff rates, applicable to a relatively large portion of Polish imports, does in fact entail a much greater revolution in the domestic market place than does, in the EU market place, the freeing from tariffs of a part only of the 1.5 per cent of goods exported to the twelve.   One might also add that in the overwhelming majority the items imported from the European Union are highly competitive compared with those goods locally manufactured and as such they pose a considerable danger to Polish enterprises.

The idea of the *Europe Agreement* was to facilitate a growth in Poland's exports, thanks to a wider access to the integrated market. The possibilities of export are, however, to a large degree determined by the structure of production. The profile of Polish tradable goods is, like the structure of production, rather traditional.   The situation is further complicated by the fact that those branches of industry that would otherwise be most competitive are precisely those most protected by the Community. This applies above all to the group of industries defined as "sensitive".   In 1993 their share of exports to the European market amounted to 49.3 per cent, while the rest of Polish exports to the countries of the Community consists of other goods, such as chemicals, machinery, or transportation equipment (around 22 per cent), which are characterised by low levels of competitiveness. All the above groups are subject to special treatment; the pace of reduction of duties on them is the slowest.   Thus it is difficult to imagine a situation where Poland's economy may be dynamized on the basis of an expansion of exports that constitute an insignificant fraction of a trade profile made up of goods whose competitiveness is, in any case, lower than those of the Community.

Another sphere where a conflict of interests between Poland and the Union emerges is agriculture. The obsolete structure of the economy is responsible for the fact that the proportion of agriculture in GDP is as high as 6.8 per cent, whereas the average for the Community is below 3 per cent.

As in other countries of the Visegrad group, Polish agriculture is characterised by a production structure which EU countries are most strenuous in protecting themselves against. It is dominated by grain production as well as beef, milk and dairy products, sugar and rapeseed. Entry into the Union by the six countries of Central and Eastern Europe would mean an increase in agricultural area of 53 per cent, in the stock of cows of 53 per cent, and of pigs by 53 per cent. If the Common Agricultural Policy were to be extended so as to include the Visegrad countries it would cost the Union $47 billion annually, while at present the agricultural budget of the Union amounts to ECU 36 billion (around $39 billion). Such an enormous increase in expenditure is obviously impossible; therefore, it has been suggested that within the framework of reform of the CAP national budgets should take over a considerable part of the financing of the direct payments.[8] Yet the chances of Poland pursuing such a policy are limited. As research indicates, an increase in the efficiency of Polish agriculture and an adjustment of prices for agricultural produce to the level of those of the European Union would entail an increase in the costs of subsidising exports (in order to eliminate surpluses) so as to reach ECU 2.4 billion, that is twenty times more than the budget of the Agricultural Market Agency (Agencja Rynku Rolnego), which is the institution financing this type of activity in Poland. Certain hopes do arise, however, as to possible changes in agricultural policy both in the countries of the European Union and in Poland as a result of the resolutions of the GATT Uruguay Round.

A review of merely part of the resolutions of the *Europe Agreement* reveals a number of problems and places a question-mark over the above-mentioned concept of the asymmetry of benefits. It is already feared that European Union producers will gain more as a consequence of the creation of the free trade zone than the supposedly privileged associated countries and this in spite of the average 18 per cent customs duty on goods imported from the European Union, and the 5.5 per cent average customs duty on industrial imports from Poland. The more limited benefits result not only from weaker competitiveness but also from the lower degree of protection of the Polish market. Poland does not apply quantitative restrictions for agricultural produce. This is why, confronted by a highly developed Western European agriculture, strongly protected as it is by the CAP, and beset by a lack of progress as regards competitiveness in prices and quality, Polish agricultural products cannot stand a chance of conquering Western markets. Food producers are also fighting a losing battle for consumers in the domestic market. Such a state of affairs only fuels the arguments in favour of protectionism. It was precisely such attitudes that urged, during 1994, the Polish government to introduce agricultural levies. A growing trade deficit between Poland and the Union has also been pinpointed by opponents of liberalization. According to GUS estimates, which differ from European estimates, the trade deficit increased from $813.9 billion in 1992 to $1,833.6 billion in 1993.

The *Europe Agreement* provides for a certain level of protection for

Polish producers. Various forms of protectionism on both sides (allowed for by GATT) are accepted in situations where:

1   imports may entail considerable losses for producers;
2   imports may lead to disturbances in certain regions or branches of the economy;
3   import threaten the stability of the balance of payments;

Moreover the Polish side alone can apply certain instruments of protection, limited in time, when the need exists for the protection of:

4   newly created branches of industry (infant industries) which should be protected until they reach a certain maturity which would allow them to face the challenges of competition,
5   sectors of the economy in the process of restructuring or in serious difficulties particularly with regard to social problems.

The possibilities of applying protectionism are, however, transitional in character. In accordance with a decision of the European Union summit in Corfu in June 1994, the Commission submitted a document to the Council of Ministers of the European Union regarding the further development of relations with the associated countries. The document provides for complex measures aimed at preparing the countries of Central Europe for membership of the Union.[9]

The first step in this direction is to limit the extent of state assistance. Emphasis is given to the need for steps to control this form of help as well as limiting its scope. Each associated country should empower a specific authority to monitor as well as control state aid and this should comply with the requirements of the *European Agreements* and be potentially comparable with Article 92 of the Treaty of Rome. Together with the Commission each of the associated countries should review its methods of state assistance and update them in such a way that they are based on principles which operate in the Community. It is advisable to consider the varieties of state assistance and their possible limitations against the background of the economic situation in each associated country.

After a certain period of time the extent of the help dispensed should be comparable to that characteristic of the Union. If satisfactory, the introduction of the principles governing the policies of competition and state assistance, as well as the implementation of part of the legal regulations of the Community will eliminate unfair competition and allow the Union to introduce a gradual reduction in customs duties on industrial articles. However, the principal problem to emerge in connection with these plans is whether the transitional period of protectionism will be long enough for the Polish economy to manage to prepare itself to successfully compete with European firms.

Poland and the Maastricht criteria

The distance between Poland and the European Union may also widen in view of the fact that the member states are at this very moment in the process of making particularly intensive efforts towards the deepening of integration, the principles of which have been specified inter alia in the Treaty on European Union, often referred to as the Maastricht Treaty. The Monetary Union may materialise through the introduction of the single currency, the ECU, aimed mainly at the elimination of costs resulting from monetary operations. A country that is a candidate for monetary union must however meet strictly specified conditions. These include:

1 price stability; the index of inflation should not exceed 1.5 per cent of the average exhibited in the previous year by the three countries with the lowest inflation rate;
2 the budget deficit should not exceed 3 per cent of GDP,
3 the national debt should be no greater than 60 per cent of GDP;
4 the average medium and long term interest rates must be stable and must not exceed by more than 2 per cent the average exhibited by the three "best" countries;
5 the mutual fluctuations in the rates of exchange should not violate the European Exchange Rate Mechanism.

At the present moment only one country meets all the requirements. The distance which Poland would have to bridge in order to join the Union is particularly great, above all as regards the level of inflation.

The retail prices index in the first three quarters of 1994 showed an average rise of about 30 per cent (with 27 per cent initially predicted by the government for 1994), while the corresponding index for the countries of the twelve was 3.1 per cent. The three countries with the lowest inflation rates (Denmark, France, and Ireland) had average prices growth of 2.8 per cent. This, increased by 1.5 (as specified in

Maastricht) gives a figure of 4.2 per cent which marks the threshold for entering the Union.

In 1995 the government expects inflation in Poland to fall to a level of 17 per cent. The budget deficit, which in 1992 amounted to 6 per cent, is expected to have fallen to 4.5 per cent in 1994, while in 1995 its reduction is expected to be sustained and reach a level of 3 per cent. The national debt amounted to 85 per cent of GDP, while interest rates for rediscount credits were 37 per cent. The exchange rate of the złoty depreciates steadily in a crawling-peg arrangement vis-a-vis a basket of main trading partners. During 1994 the monthly rate of depreciation was reduced on two occasions: in September it was cut from 1.6 to 1.5 per cent and in November to 1.4 per cent.

Table 10.1
The economic situation of Poland in 1993 as measured against the Maastricht criteria

Inflation rate	
average annual %	35.3
Budget deficit	
% of GDP	4.5
National debt	
% of GDP	85.0
Interest rate	
rediscount rate	35.4
Exchange rate	
crawling-peg mechanism	
monthly depreciation rate %	
at 11 November 1994	1.4

Sources: Biuletyn Statystyczny, (GUS, Warsaw); *National Bank of Poland*, 1994

Despite the considerable pace of prices growth in Poland very positive changes are at present evident in production growth and economic revitalization. The pace of GDP growth has been sustained at a level of 4.5 per cent and a certain improvement has been observed in the labour market. In 1994 unemployment stabilised at a level of 16.6 per cent. But strong growth in the domestic market also stimulates demand for imported goods thus posing a danger as regards a worsening of the trade deficit, already high due to structural reasons. With respect to the pace of economic growth in 1994 Poland occupied one of the top places in Europe.

Institutional, political and social problems

The discrepancies between Poland and the Union also manifest themselves on the institutional level. The smooth functioning of a market economy and a democratic system is impossible without well organised institutional back-up, which, in Poland, is still taking shape. The underdevelopment of the banking sector, financial institutions and firms which provide consultative services and act as intermediaries in establishing contacts still constitutes a significant obstacle in the way of economic growth.

Another factor which limits the scope of reforms in Poland is the high social cost they entail. Society expects a rapid increase in the standard of living. The peculiarity of this situation needs to be understood: while many people in Poland used to equate the idea of regaining national sovereignty with a rapid increase in the standard of living, the latter has been increasing at an unusually slow pace, being accompanied by social pathologies which in the conditions of the communist economy were not perceived on such a massive scale. This applies above all to the drastic increase in unemployment.[10] At the same time Polish society has exhibited a considerable demand for imported goods, mainly resulting from the liberalization of trade as well as the general accessibility of goods in the market. The complete opening of the frontiers has made the people aware of the difference in the level of development between Poland and the countries of Western Europe.

Obviously, consumers' aspirations, if unfulfilled, breed social discontent, which poses a serious threat to the reform process. This factor deserves special consideration because in the postwar history of Poland social pressure has often forced the authorities into concessions. In addition, there is a widespread misapprehension that governments can and should submit to consumers' demands. Polish society is conscious of its power. Unlike the former Czechoslovakia, the revolution in Poland cannot be described as "velvet" in character. Changes in the way of government were won in the course of mass protests and struggles which, though stifled, lasted for decades, finally leading to success. Thus an upsurge of social discontent can threaten the reforms and result in their slow down.

The behaviour of various lobbies and their influence on political parties is also a cause for concern. Many parties are already aware of the fact that excessively austere reforms can cause a loss of popularity. By way of example, it has been estimated that a radical restructuring of agriculture would cost the peasants' parties 75 per cent of their electorate. Thus it is not surprising that some politicians from the Polish Peasants' Party exhibit an uncompromising stance, claiming that agriculture, as a particularly important area of production, cannot be made to suffer as a result of political compromise. Given the context of such declarations there are serious misgivings as to whether a genuine reform of Polish agriculture will prove successful. Generally speaking however society's attitude towards Poland's integration into the European Union is positive. Opinion polls have indicated that as much as 79 per cent of Polish society supports Poland's full membership of the Union (28 per cent of those questioned are "decidedly for" the idea, while 51 per cent are "rather in favour" of it). Most concern over Poland's entry into the Union is generated by the situation of Polish agriculture (24 per cent of those questioned predict the collapse of individual holdings in Poland) as well as by the condition of state-owned companies.

Objectivity does not allow one to disregard problems the Union may envisage as resulting from the possibility of the countries of Central and Eastern Europe being integrated into its structures. The potential membership of those countries engenders immense anxiety and protests among Europe's farmers as well as the inhabitants of the least developed regions. This results from well-grounded fears that the benefits that some groups are presently enjoying might be withdrawn in favour of those even less well off.

Serious problems can also arise from the principle of the free movement of people. Present estimates indicate that 3-6 million citizens from the Visegrad group would like to emigrate to the West. Such an enormous influx of people could result in serious difficulties in the markets of the Union and exacerbate the existing problems of labour.

The reforms would also require changes in the voting system in the Union's Council of Ministers. Were the present system of voting to be maintained the newly admitted countries of the Visegrad group would have at their disposal more votes than the four less developed countries of the Community (Spain, Portugal, Ireland and Greece) which would exert considerable influence on Union policy.

Taking stock of achievements

A casual review of the problems facing the Polish economy in its process of adjustment to the requirements of the Union gives rise to concern as to the possibility of a full integration into its structures. However, one must not forget the immense transformations which that economy has already undergone, transformations unprecedented in economic history. Of paramount importance is Poland's rejoining the family of democratic states. This is an unquestionable fact in spite of a considerable fragmentation of the Polish political spectrum particularly on the right.

Many reforms have also been implemented, changing the character of the economy from one that was centrally planned to one that is market-oriented. Among these the following were of crucial importance:

1   the abolition of price controls. It was only five years ago that prices in Poland were controlled and completely divorced from production and costs. There was also a policy of wide ranging state subsidies for goods and consumer services;[11]
2   the initiation of a policy of wide ranging privatization. This has made possible a change in the ownership structure of enterprises, as well as an increase in the efficiency of production and some rationalization in manufacturing structure;[12]
3   the introduction of the internal convertibility of the złoty. This has made possible a confrontation of the domestic price system with world prices, just as it has made it possible for the first time in recent years to assess the competitiveness of the Polish economy;
4   changes in the legal system. Between November 1990 and September 1993 over 50 per cent of the legal regulations valid in Poland underwent change. Pressure of time resulted, unfortunately, in numerous imperfections arising from loop-holes and the lack of precision and clarity. Laws being passed in such a form is still the lesser of two evils: in spite of their flaws they are better than the old ones. Since March 1994 a requirement has been in place (following a decree of the Council of Ministers) calling for all drafts of legal acts which are submitted to the Council of Ministers to be accompanied by an expert assessment of their compliance with European law.[13] The scale of acceleration can best be illustrated by the fact that in the last three years 200 legal acts have been assessed, almost 100 of them in the last few months of 1994;
5   the creation of programmes for support and protection of competition. In the postwar history of Poland the idea of market competition was practically nonexistent; it is only now that a proper climate for its development is being engendered. Enterprises were protected by an artificial system of prices, protectionism in trade,

state subsidies and subventions. A government programme for the development of competition has been worked out, which has been approved by the Council of Ministers. In this document the main stumbling blocks for the development of competition have been identified as have the objectives of competition policy and the assumptions on which they are based. For the fostering of a proper climate of competition in Poland the following tasks have been specified:

- creation of small and medium-sized businesses
- creation and implementation of antitrust regulations
- reduction in the scope of price interventionism
- improvement in enterprises' access to credit
- reduction of import restrictions

The regulation of the principles of competition has also brought about changes in the relevant sections of civil law;

6   the reform of the taxation system in Poland, which consisted in the introduction of value-added tax as already obligatory throughout the Union, as well as excise duties. Changes in the taxation system in Poland are taking place in accordance with the basic principles of the Union, resulting in a uniform system of taxation for all legal entities (regardless of the form of ownership, structure etc.) and a tax system that does not discriminate against, nor favour, imported goods and services;

7   reforms of the banking system. Changes in the organization of banking in Poland were initiated in 1989 when a two stage system of banking was introduced: the National Bank of Poland became the Central Bank, whose main functions are the regulation of the money-supply and the extent of the liquidity of commercial banks, as well as carrying responsibility for the exchange rate. As such, it has acquired a certain sovereignty and is not obliged to yield to pressure from the government (for example as regards the amount of money issued, no decision in this respect can be reached without its consent, as that of an equal partner);

8   adjustment in accepted norms. In Poland the process of adjusting the norms and technical regulations so as to comply with those of the Union has begun;

9   adjustment of customs procedures. The introduction of the Single Administrative Document (SAD), which obtains throughout the Union, has simplified customs procedures and the formalities involved in the flow of goods; it requires the customs declaration to

encode the items according to a special system, as in the Union.

It cannot be denied that the list of achievements is an imposing one, especially in view of the fact that the above reforms are structural in character, and embrace not only the economy but also politics, institutions, the educational system, and foreign relations.

The costs of Poland's remaining outside an integrated Europe

The problem of accepting Poland and other countries of the Visegrad group to the Union has at present a mainly economic dimension, as most of the politicians and economic activists approach it in terms of the costs of the adjustments which would have to be borne by both sides. It is impossible, at least at this stage, explicitly to quantify the costs of leaving the countries of the Visegrad group, plus Bulgaria and Rumania, outside the Union. Yet it can be stated with full certainty that such a cost will have more than an economic dimension. The lack of an unambiguous stand as regards the acceptance of the states of Central and Eastern Europe into the Union has already generated disappointment among the societies of that part of the continent. A precise specification of the schedule for their integration would surely provide a stimulus for further reforms, as well as act as compensation for the costs which have so far been sustained.

Contrary to expectations, the Essen summit in December 1994 did not specify the date for the acceptance of the associated states to the Union, although Klaus Haensch, the Speaker of the European Parliament, referred to the widening of the Union as "necessary and inevitable". Yet indispensable conditions for full integration must be the completion of the reform process in the associated countries as well as a reform of the Common Agricultural Policy. The possibility of changes to the Maastricht Treaty has also been allowed for so as to enable the countries of Central and Eastern Europe to be drawn into co-operation in politics, security and domestic affairs.

In practice this may imply that the costs of adjustment will be exclusively borne by the countries aspiring to be in the Union. A widening of the economic gap between the two sides is likely to lead to an upsurge in social discontent, which in turn, can entail the threat of the rise of various undesirable nationalisms, utterly opposed to the idea of integration.

It is also impossible to imagine a scenario where further economic growth and progress towards integration would not encounter barriers created by the underdevelopment of Eastern partners. The clearest example illustrating the phenomenon of the migration of problems is the spreading of the results of environmental degradation which may threaten the member states of the Union. Exacerbation of differences in the standard of living is conducive to an increase in social pathologies, which may have particularly negative consequences for the fight against organised crime, so characteristic of the present moment.

Consequently, fostering the growth of the associated countries seems to be in the enlightened self-interest of the Western partners. Although the many years of postwar division in Europe cannot be done away with overnight the countries undergoing the process of economic transformation are entitled to radical support.[14] The widening of the Union to the East would certainly result in more foreign capital being attracted to that part of Europe which in turn would accelerate the pace of economic growth.

Notes

1   The part of the agreement referring to trade has been binding since 1992, which was possible thanks to the EC-Commission, which is empowered to take decisions relating to trade policy without prior ratification by the parliaments of the member states and the European Parliament.

2   *Europe Agreement EC-Poland.*

3   This article was written before the expansion of the twelve, and refers to the state of affairs existing at that time.

4   The sides do, however, preserve the right to pursue an independent trade policy vis-a-vis third countries. The trade between Poland and Spain and Portugal has also received separate consideration as in those countries the transitional regulations are still operational, connected with the complete adjustment of those economies to the requirements specified by the European Union.

5   Some of the goods enjoy the suspension of customs duties within quotas specified yearly, the so-called "ceilings" which are to be gradually increased by 20 per cent per year, until ultimately, in five years time, they are eliminated.

6   *Eurostat 1993.*

7   *Rocznik Statystyczny Handlu Zagranicznego 1994*, (GUS, Warsaw).

8   Richard A. Baldwin, "Ku zjednoczonej Europie" (Towards an Integrated Europe), *Europa*, No.2, 1994.

9 Communication from the Commission to the Council follow-up to the Commission Communication on "The Europe Agreements and beyond: a strategy to prepare the countries of Central and Eastern Europe for Accession", COM(94), final, 27 July 1994.

10 In the centrally planned economy there existed so-called crypto-unemployment. According to the communist phraseology, however, work was a universally accessible commodity; it was even guaranteed, although not always respected, in the relevant article of the constitution.

11 The outlays on subsidies amounted to 40 per cent of public spending. In 1990 the index of the share of the subsidies in the budget fell to 1 per cent.

12 Unfortunately the present government is clearly slowing down the process of privatization.

13 *Dziennik Ustaw*, (Journal of Legal Acts) No.11, 1993.

14 There do, however, exist programmes of assistance for the countries of Central and Eastern Europe, such as the PHARE programme, where the financial resources average $10 per citizen.

References

Biuletyn Statystyczny, (GUS, Warsaw), No., 9/94.

Gawlikowska-Hueckel, K., Zielinska-Glebocka, A., "Motivation for Protectionism in the Light of Transformation and the Europe Agreement", Florence 1993.

Gazeta Bankowa, No 46, 1994.

Mały Rocznik Statystyczny 1994, (GUS, Warsaw).

Mayhew, A., "Future policy of the European Union towards the countries of Central and Eastern Europe", in *Transformation and Integration in Europe*, Gdańsk 1994.

Zielińska-Głębocka, A., "Poland's Commercial Adjustment In the Light of the Evolution of Integrational Processes in Europe", Gdańsk 1994.